Creepy & Creative:

100 Fun Halloween Recipes for Kids and Families

By Josephine S. Stell

Copyright © 2024 by Josephine S. Stell

The recipes, tips, and techniques presented in this book are original works created by the author. Every effort has been made to ensure the accuracy of the information and instructions provided. However, the publisher and the author assume no responsibility for errors or omissions or for any consequences of the use of the information contained herein. All trademarks, product names, and brand names used in this book are the property of their respective owners. The mention of any specific product, service, or third-party organization does not imply endorsement by the author or publisher.

The content in this cookbook is intended for informational and educational purposes only. While every effort has been made to provide accurate and safe cooking instructions, readers are responsible for their own safety when preparing recipes and handling food.

The author and publisher make no guarantees regarding the results of the recipes, and individual results may vary based on factors such as ingredient quality, cooking equipment, and personal skill level. Always exercise caution when using kitchen appliances, sharp utensils, or potentially allergenic ingredients. It is recommended to thoroughly check all ingredients for any food allergies or dietary restrictions before attempting a recipe.

The nutritional information provided in this book, if any, is based on general estimates and should not be considered precise. Please consult with a registered dietitian or nutritionist for more specific dietary advice. The author and publisher are not responsible for any adverse effects or consequences resulting from the use of the information or recipes provided in this book.

Table of Contents:

Introduction:

Welcome, dear friends, to a culinary adventure that promises to add a dash of mystery and a sprinkle of magic to your Halloween festivities. This is not just any cookbook; it's a delightful journey into a world where creativity knows no bounds, and the kitchen becomes a playground for both young and old. As we embark on this enchanting expedition together, I invite you to embrace the spirit of Halloween with open arms and open hearts, transforming your kitchen into a cauldron of creativity and fun.

In "Creepy & Creative: 100 Fun Halloween Recipes for Kids and Families," you will discover a treasure trove of recipes that are as delightful to prepare as they are to devour. Our culinary voyage is designed to captivate the imaginations of children and adults alike, making Halloween a celebration not just of spooks and scares, but of family togetherness and gastronomic delight. Imagine the joy on your little one's face as they shape Witch's Finger Cookies or the laughter shared as you create a bubbling Witch's Brew Punch. This collection is meant to be a catalyst for creating cherished memories.

Each recipe in this book has been meticulously crafted with you in mind, ensuring that even the most novice kitchen witches and wizards can conjure up deliciously spooky treats. With step-by-step instructions and tips for adding creative, eerie decorations, you'll find that each dish is transformed into a work of art. From appetizers that will send shivers down your spine to desserts that glow with ghostly charm, these recipes are sure to enchant every member of your family.

Our journey begins with Appetizers & Snacks, where you'll find bewitching delights like Ghostly Guacamole Dip and Eerie Eyeball Deviled Eggs. These are perfect for setting the tone of your Halloween gathering, tantalizing taste buds with flavors that are as mysterious as they are delicious. Imagine serving a platter of Creepy Crawly Cheese Balls, each one bearing a sinister grin, or delighting guests with Mummy Jalapeño Poppers wrapped in their pastry bandages. Each bite is a step further into the enchanting world of Halloween.

As we move into Main Dishes, prepare to be spellbound by recipes that turn ordinary meals into extraordinary experiences. Picture a bubbling Witch's Cauldron Chili that warms the soul, or Jack-O'-Lantern Pizzas that bring a smile to every ghoul and goblin at the table. These dishes, including the Spooky Spaghetti and Eyeballs, are designed to be hearty and satisfying, ensuring your family is well-fed as they embark on their Halloween adventures.

Desserts, of course, are where our creativity truly takes flight. Let your imagination run wild with Creepy Crawly Cupcakes or indulge in the rich, chocolaty embrace of a Ghostly Gooey Brownie. Each dessert is an opportunity to engage children in the kitchen, allowing them to express their creativity as they decorate and design their own edible masterpieces. Their eyes will light up with delight as they create Skull Sugar Cookies or assemble Graveyard Dirt Cups.

No Halloween feast would be complete without a selection of spooky Drinks, and our collection is sure to impress. From the refreshing Ghoul's Grape Fizz to the warming comfort of Haunted Hot Chocolate, there's a potion for every palate. These concoctions, like the Vampire's Blood Mocktail, add a touch of whimsy and wonder, making them perfect for toasting to a night of fun and fright.

Finally, we explore Breakfast & Brunch, ensuring that your Halloween celebrations extend from dawn to dusk. Start your day with a Creepy Crawly Pancake or a Monster Muffin, setting the stage for a day of spooky festivities.

Join me in the kitchen, where together we will transform simple ingredients into magical memories. Whether you're hosting a Halloween party or simply enjoying time with your family, "Creepy & Creative: 100 Fun Halloween Recipes for Kids and Families" is your guide to a spook-tacular celebration. Happy haunting, and may your Halloween be filled with laughter, love, and delicious delights!

1. Bewitching Bat Wings

Amidst the flickering candlelight and the rustling of autumn leaves, a culinary spell awaits. Gently conjured, these Bewitching Bat Wings possess a delightful charm to captivate both young ghouls and seasoned witches alike, offering a taste of magic and mystery at your Halloween table.

Preparation time: 15 minutes
Cooking time: 35 minutes
Ready-in time: 50 minutes
Serving size: 4 people

Ingredients:
2 pounds chicken wings, tips removed
1/2 cup soy sauce
1/4 cup honey
1 tablespoon apple cider vinegar
1 tablespoon minced garlic
1 teaspoon ground ginger
1/2 teaspoon black pepper
1/4 teaspoon cayenne pepper
1 tablespoon sesame oil
Black food coloring (optional)
Sesame seeds for garnish
Chopped green onions for garnish

Instructions:

First, let's create a potion that will infuse our wings with flavor. In a large mixing bowl, combine the soy sauce, honey, apple cider vinegar, minced garlic, ground ginger, black pepper, and cayenne pepper. If you're feeling a bit adventurous, add a few drops of black food coloring to enhance the mystique of your bat wings.

Now, place your chicken wings into this enchanting marinade, ensuring each wing is well-coated with the potion. Allow them to luxuriate in this bath for at least 15 minutes—though, if time allows, a longer marination will deepen their flavor.

As the wings absorb their magical essence, preheat your oven to a bewitching 400°F (200°C). Line a baking sheet with parchment paper or foil, and gently brush it with a whisper of sesame oil to prevent sticking.

Once your wings are adequately steeped, arrange them on the prepared baking sheet, ensuring they lay in a single layer for even cooking. Into the oven, they go, baking for approximately 35 minutes, or until they achieve a crisp and caramelized exterior that promises a delightful crunch.

With the wings now cooked to perfection, remove them from the oven and let them rest for a moment before serving. Sprinkle with sesame seeds and a dusting of chopped green onions to add a final touch of enchantment.

Gather your creatures of the night and savor these spellbinding wings, a perfect accompaniment to tales of specters and spooks. As the last morsel disappears, let the magic linger in the air, and may your Halloween be filled with delightful frights and flavors!

2. Ghostly Guacamole Dip

In the spirit of Halloween's enchanting mystery, let's transform the humble avocado into a ghoulishly delightful dip that will charm both young and old alike. Gather your little goblins and witches, for this recipe promises not just flavor, but a dash of spooky fun!

Preparation time: 10 minutes
Cooking time: None
Ready-in time: 10 minutes
Serving size: 4 people

Ingredients:
3 ripe avocados
1 lime, juiced
1 small red onion, finely chopped
1 small tomato, deseeded and diced
2 tablespoons fresh cilantro, chopped
1 clove garlic, minced
1/2 teaspoon salt
1/4 teaspoon cayenne pepper
1-2 tablespoons sour cream
1/4 cup black olives, sliced
A pinch of paprika (for garnish)

Instructions:

First, let's invite the avocados to the party. Cut them in half, remove the pits, and scoop the creamy goodness into a bowl. Give them a good mash with a fork, leaving it a little chunky for texture. Now, squeeze the juice of a lime over the avocados; this not only adds zest but keeps our dip vibrant and green.

Next, add in the finely chopped red onion and diced tomato. These will give our dip a delightful crunch and burst of color. Toss in the chopped cilantro for that fresh herbal note. To spice things up, add the minced garlic, salt, and a pinch of cayenne pepper. Stir everything together until the flavors are well acquainted.

For the ghostly touch, swirl in the sour cream until it forms eerie white streaks through the guacamole. It's now time for the final flourish: arrange the sliced black olives on top to resemble spooky eyes peering out from the green depths.

Finally, sprinkle a touch of paprika for a hauntingly beautiful finish. Serve with your favorite tortilla chips or fresh veggie sticks, and watch as your guests dive into this ghoulish delight.

May your gatherings be filled with laughter and just the right amount of fright. Remember, every great dish is a story waiting to be shared, so let this ghostly guacamole be the haunting tale you tell this Halloween!

3. Creepy Crawly Cheese Balls

When the autumn leaves start to fall, the kitchen becomes a haven of playful culinary creations. These Creepy Crawly Cheese Balls are not only frightfully fun but also delightfully delicious, making them the perfect addition to your Halloween festivities.

Preparation time: 20 minutes
Cooking time: 10 minutes
Ready-in time: 30 minutes
Serving size: 4 people

Ingredients:
8 ounces of cream cheese, softened
1 cup sharp cheddar cheese, shredded
1 tablespoon Worcestershire sauce
1 teaspoon garlic powder
Salt and pepper, to taste
1 cup crushed pretzels
16 pretzel sticks
32 black olives
16 cherry tomatoes
Fresh parsley for garnish

Instructions:

Let's embark on this culinary adventure by first taking our softened cream cheese and placing it in a mixing bowl. Add in the shredded cheddar cheese, Worcestershire sauce, and garlic powder. Give it a gentle mix until everything is well combined, and don't forget to season with a pinch of salt and pepper.

Now, the magic begins as we form the mixture into small, round balls. Aim for about the size of a golf ball. Once rolled, set them aside as we prepare their crunchy coating. Take your crushed pretzels and place them on a shallow plate. Roll each cheese ball in the pretzel crumbs, ensuring they are covered evenly, giving them a delightful crunch with every bite.

To create the creepy crawly effect, gently insert two pretzel sticks into each cheese ball to form the legs. Next, for the eyes, slice the black olives in half and attach them with a dab of cream cheese. Use the cherry tomatoes, halved, to create little noses that will have everyone giggling with frightful delight.

Finally, arrange our little creatures on a platter, garnishing with fresh parsley to add a touch of earthy elegance.

Gather around, dear friends and family, and enjoy these delightful bites of spooky fun. As the candles flicker and the laughter echoes, these cheese balls will surely become a cherished memory of your Halloween celebrations. Bon appétit!

4. Spooky Spider Crackers

As the moon casts eerie shadows on Halloween night, transform a simple snack into a spine-tingling treat. Perfectly creepy and delightfully delicious, these spider crackers are sure to add a touch of magic and mischief to your festive gatherings.

Preparation time: 10 minutes
Cooking time: 0 minutes
Ready-in time: 10 minutes
Serving size: 4 people

Ingredients:
16 round crackers
8 tablespoons cream cheese, softened
8 black olives, sliced
32 pretzel sticks
16 small candy eyes

Instructions:

Begin by gathering your little ghouls and goblins around the kitchen counter. Spread a generous tablespoon of creamy cheese onto eight of the crackers, ensuring every inch is covered with this delicious layer. Place another cracker on top, sandwiching the cream cheese snugly in between.

Next, let's craft the spider legs! Snap each pretzel stick in half, so you have sixteen pieces. Insert four pretzel halves into the cream cheese on each side of every sandwich, forming the spindly legs that will delight (and perhaps spook) your little ones.

Now, it's time to bring your spider to life. Gently press two olive slices onto the top of each cracker sandwich, creating round, glossy eyes. For an extra touch of whimsy, fixate the candy eyes onto the olive slices, giving your spiders a quirky, animated expression that will surely charm any Halloween table.

And there you have it—a frightfully fun and delicious snack ready to be devoured by eager hands.

"Let your Spooky Spider Crackers scuttle onto the scene, weaving their web of deliciousness at your Halloween festivities. Watch as your guests gather round, charmed by these edible critters, weaving a spell of fun and flavor that's simply enchanting.

5. Mummy Jalapeño Poppers

As the shadows lengthen and the moon casts its eerie glow, our kitchens become the stage for delightfully ghoulish treats. These Mummy Jalapeño Poppers are a frightfully fun way to add a bit of playful spookiness to your Halloween festivities.

Preparation time: 15 minutes
Cooking time: 20 minutes
Ready-in time: 35 minutes
Serving size: 4 people

Ingredients:
8 large jalapeño peppers
4 ounces cream cheese, softened
1 cup shredded cheddar cheese
1 teaspoon garlic powder
1 teaspoon onion powder
1/2 teaspoon smoked paprika
1/4 teaspoon salt
1/4 teaspoon black pepper
1 sheet puff pastry, thawed
1 egg, beaten
16 candy eyes

Instructions:

First, my dear friends, we must prepare the jalapeños by slicing them in half lengthwise and carefully removing the seeds and membranes. This ensures a delightful balance of spice without overwhelming our taste buds. In a mixing bowl, combine the softened cream cheese, shredded cheddar, garlic powder, onion powder, smoked paprika, salt, and pepper. Give it a good stir until everything is beautifully melded together.

Now, we take our puff pastry and, using a sharp knife or pizza cutter, slice it into thin strips, approximately 1/4 inch wide. These will become the wrappings for our mummies.

Fill each jalapeño half with the cheese mixture, making sure to fill them generously. Then, lovingly wrap each filled jalapeño with the puff pastry strips, leaving a little space to add those adorable candy eyes after baking.

Next, preheat your oven to 400°F (200°C). Place the wrapped jalapeños on a baking sheet lined with parchment paper. Brush each mummy with the beaten egg, giving them a lovely golden hue as they bake. Pop them into the oven for about 20 minutes, or until the pastry is golden and crispy.

Once baked, remove them from the oven and let them cool for a few minutes. Finally, press two candy eyes into the melted cheese of each mummy, bringing them to life in the most delightfully spooky way.

And there you have it, a dish that promises both a fright and a feast! These whimsical mummies are sure to cast a spell over your Halloween gathering, leaving both young and old enchanted by their taste and charm. Enjoy every spooky bite, and remember, the magic is in the details!

6. Phantom Popcorn Balls

On a night when the moon is full and the air is crisp, gather your little goblins around the kitchen counter for a spooky treat-making session. These Phantom Popcorn Balls are sure to delight with their ghostly charm and sweet surprise in every bite.

Preparation time: 15 minutes
Cooking time: 10 minutes
Ready-in time: 25 minutes
Serving size: 4 people

Ingredients:
8 cups popped popcorn
1 cup mini marshmallows
1/2 cup light corn syrup
1/2 cup granulated sugar
1/4 cup unsalted butter
1 teaspoon vanilla extract
1/4 teaspoon salt
Assorted candy eyes or sprinkles for decoration

Instructions:

Begin by preparing your popcorn. Make sure it's freshly popped, light, and airy. Place these fluffy kernels in a large mixing bowl and set them aside. In a medium saucepan, combine the mini marshmallows, light corn syrup, sugar, and unsalted butter. Stir over medium heat until the butter melts and the mixture begins to simmer gently.

As the sweet concoction bubbles softly, add in the vanilla extract and a pinch of salt. Stir until everything is well blended and the marshmallows have completely dissolved. This fragrant mixture will serve as the glue for your popcorn balls.

Now, pour the hot syrup carefully over the popcorn. Use a spatula to gently fold the popcorn into the syrup until every piece is well coated. It's a sticky business, but oh, what fun it is! Let the mixture cool slightly, just enough to handle comfortably.

With slightly buttered hands, form the sticky popcorn into eight evenly-sized balls. Press them firmly but gently, so they hold together without crushing the popcorn. Decorate each ball with candy eyes or sprinkles, giving them a ghostly visage. Allow them to set on a parchment-lined tray before serving.

Ah, the magic of these Phantom Popcorn Balls! They disappear as quickly as a ghost in the night, but their sugary spell will linger on. Gather around, dear friends, and enjoy the sweet enchantment of Halloween!

7. Ghoulish Garlic Knots

As the autumn leaves crunch underfoot and a ghostly breeze whispers through the trees, it's the perfect time to gather the family for a cozy kitchen adventure. These Ghoulish Garlic Knots bring a spirited twist to a classic delight, adding a hint of spooky charm to your Halloween celebrations.

Preparation time: 20 minutes
Cooking time: 15 minutes
Ready-in time: 35 minutes
Serving size: 4 people

Ingredients:
2 cups all-purpose flour
1 tablespoon sugar
1 packet (2 1/4 teaspoons) instant yeast
3/4 teaspoon salt
3/4 cup warm water (about 110°F)
3 tablespoons olive oil, divided
4 cloves garlic, minced
2 tablespoons unsalted butter, melted
1 tablespoon fresh parsley, chopped
1/4 teaspoon red pepper flakes (optional)
1/4 cup grated Parmesan cheese

Instructions:

Welcome to our bewitching kitchen! Let's begin by whisking together the flour, sugar, yeast, and salt in a large mixing bowl. Add the warm water and two tablespoons of olive oil, then stir until the mixture forms a soft dough. Now, it's time for a little elbow grease—knead the dough on a lightly floured surface for about 5 minutes until it's smooth and elastic.

Place your dough in a lightly oiled bowl, cover it with a clean kitchen towel, and let it rise in a warm spot for about 15 minutes. While the dough is resting, let's prepare our tantalizing garlic butter. In a small saucepan over low heat, combine the remaining tablespoon of olive oil with the minced garlic, stirring gently for 1-2 minutes until fragrant. Remove from heat and mix in the melted butter, parsley, and red pepper flakes.

Once the dough has risen, divide it into 8 equal pieces. Roll each piece into a rope, about 8 inches long, and tie it into a loose knot. Arrange the knots on a parchment-lined baking sheet, giving them room to puff up in the oven. Brush each knot generously with your aromatic garlic butter, and sprinkle the Parmesan cheese over the top.

Bake in a preheated oven at 375°F for 12-15 minutes, until golden brown and delightfully fragrant. Let the knots cool slightly before serving—if you can resist the temptation!

With these Ghoulish Garlic Knots, your Halloween table will bewitch all who gather around. As these delightful treats disappear, remember, the joy of cooking together is the most magical ingredient of all. Until next time, may your kitchen be filled with laughter and love!

8. Eerie Eyeball Deviled Eggs

In the spirit of a spooky Halloween soirée, let us dive into a dish that teeters between the whimsical and the wicked—a devilishly delightful treat that is sure to mesmerize your little goblins and witches. Imagine a platter of eggs transformed into eerie eyeballs, gazing mysteriously from your table.

Preparation time: 20 minutes
Cooking time: 10 minutes
Ready-in time: 30 minutes
Serving size: 4 people

Ingredients:
6 large eggs
3 tablespoons mayonnaise
1 teaspoon Dijon mustard
1/2 teaspoon white vinegar
Salt and freshly ground black pepper, to taste
Green olives with pimentos, sliced
Red food coloring
Paprika, for dusting

Instructions:

Begin by placing the eggs in a saucepan, covering them with cold water by about an inch. Bring the water to a rolling boil over medium-high heat, then remove from heat, covering with a lid. Let the eggs sit for about 10 minutes. Once the time is up, transfer them to a bowl of ice water to cool.

Now, gently peel the eggs and slice them lengthwise. Be sure to handle them with care! Scoop out the yolks and place them in a medium bowl. Mash the yolks with a fork until they are crumbled to perfection.

To this sunny mixture, add mayonnaise, Dijon mustard, white vinegar, a pinch of salt, and a dash of pepper. Stir until everything is smooth and creamy. Taste and adjust your seasonings as you see fit.

Next, it's time to bring these eggs to life! Spoon the yolk mixture back into the egg whites, filling each hollow graciously. Now for the eerie details—place a slice of green olive right in the center of each yolk mound, creating the pupil of our spooky eyeball.

To heighten the eeriness, use a toothpick dipped in red food coloring to draw small squiggly lines extending from the olive outward, mimicking bloodshot veins. For a final touch, sprinkle a light dusting of paprika over the tops to give them a ghostly glow.

Display them on a platter, and watch as they become the centerpiece of your Halloween gathering!

Ah, the charm of a Halloween feast lies in the details, where each bite is a playful nod to the fantastical. May these eyes keep watch over your party, ensuring all who gather are delightfully spooked and splendidly satisfied.

9. Vampire Veggie Platter

As the moon casts its eerie glow and shadows dance across the walls, it's time to summon a dish that brings a playful fright to your Halloween spread. This Vampire Veggie Platter isn't just a feast for the eyes—it's a deliciously ghoulish treat that tempts even the pickiest little vampires.

Preparation time: 20 minutes
Cooking time: 0 minutes
Ready-in time: 20 minutes
Serving size: 4 people

Ingredients:
1 red bell pepper
1 yellow bell pepper
1 cucumber
1 bunch of radishes
1 bunch of baby carrots
1 cup cherry tomatoes
1 small head of broccoli
1 cup hummus
1/4 cup black olives
1/4 cup sliced almonds

Instructions:

Let's begin crafting our spooky masterpiece by cutting the red and yellow bell peppers in half, removing the seeds, and slicing them into long, thin strips. These will form the fiery fangs of our vampire creation. Next, slice the cucumber into rounds, each representing the scales of our vegetable creature.

Now, take the radishes and carve them into small, jagged teeth—be careful not to slice them too thinly, as you want them to maintain their bite. Arrange the baby carrots on the platter to mimic the outstretched claws of our vampire. Cherry tomatoes, with their vibrant red hue, will serve as the ominous eyes peering from the shadows.

Break the broccoli into small florets, scattering them across the platter like a dark forest. Then, in the center, gently place a bowl of creamy hummus, which will serve as the heart of this eerie ensemble.

For a finishing touch, slice the black olives into rings and sprinkle them across the platter for a hint of mystery. Top with a scattering of sliced almonds to add an unexpected crunch, reminiscent of bat wings flapping in the night.

And there you have it—a Vampire Veggie Platter that is as captivating as it is nutritious.

Now, my dear friends, as you and your little goblins delve into this platter of frightful delights, remember that the true magic of Halloween lies in the joy of sharing. Here's to a spooktacular gathering filled with laughter, love, and a touch of delicious mischief!

10. Monster Mash Hummus

In the spirit of Halloween, let the ghoulish green of this delightful hummus bring a touch of fun and fright to your festive spread. Perfect for little monsters and their families, this whimsical dip will have everyone howling for more as they scoop up the vibrant flavor with their favorite veggies or spooky crackers.

Preparation time: 15 minutes
Cooking time: 0 minutes
Ready-in time: 15 minutes
Serving size: 4 people

Ingredients:
1 can (15 ounces) chickpeas, drained and rinsed
1/4 cup fresh lemon juice (about 1 large lemon)
1/4 cup tahini
1 small clove of garlic, minced
2 tablespoons olive oil, plus more for serving
1/2 teaspoon ground cumin
Salt to taste
2 to 3 tablespoons water
1/2 cup fresh spinach leaves, packed
1/4 cup canned pumpkin puree
Black sesame seeds, for garnish

Instructions:

Now, gather your brave ingredients and prepare to blend a monstrous masterpiece. Begin by placing the chickpeas, lemon juice, tahini, garlic, olive oil, cumin, and a pinch of salt into the bowl of a food processor. Pulse the mixture for about 30 seconds, then scrape down the sides and bottom of the bowl to ensure everything is thoroughly mixed.

Next, add the spinach leaves to give your hummus that eerie green hue. Pulse again until the spinach is well incorporated, and the blend becomes a smooth, ghastly green paste. Should the hummus appear too thick, carefully add a tablespoon of water at a time, blending until you achieve your desired consistency.

For a spooky twist, introduce the pumpkin puree into the mix, giving your hummus a subtle sweetness and a hint of Halloween magic. Pulse again until the pumpkin is fully combined, revealing a charmingly creepy shade of greenish-orange.

Transfer your Monster Mash Hummus to a serving bowl, and with a flourish, drizzle a touch of olive oil over the top. Sprinkle with black sesame seeds to complete the enchantment. Serve this devilishly delicious dip with your choice of veggies or crackers and watch your little monsters devour it with glee.

May your Halloween be filled with hauntingly good flavors, laughter, and a dash of mischief. Until next time, keep stirring up fun in the kitchen and delighting in the joy of shared meals and festive gatherings. Happy haunting, dear friends!

11. Witch's Brew Cheese Fondue

As the moon casts its eerie glow and shadows dance upon the walls, gather around a cauldron of bubbling cheese fondue. This mystical concoction, with its rich and creamy texture, is sure to enchant both young and old alike, making your Halloween gathering delightfully memorable.

Preparation time: 15 minutes
Cooking time: 15 minutes
Ready-in time: 30 minutes
Serving size: 4 people

Ingredients:
1 clove garlic, halved
1 cup dry white wine
1 tablespoon lemon juice
8 ounces Gruyère cheese, grated
8 ounces Emmental cheese, grated
1 tablespoon cornstarch
1 tablespoon kirsch (cherry brandy)
Pinch of nutmeg
Freshly ground black pepper, to taste
Cubed French bread, for dipping
Assorted vegetables, like carrots and broccoli, for dipping

Instructions:

Begin by rubbing the inside of a fondue pot or heavy saucepan with the cut side of the garlic halves. This will impart a subtle aroma and flavor to our fondue, setting the stage for a spellbinding experience. Next, pour the wine and lemon juice into the pot and warm gently over medium heat—just until the mixture begins to steam.

Now, let's work some magic with the cheese. In a large bowl, toss the grated Gruyère and Emmental with cornstarch until well coated. Gradually add the cheese to the pot, stirring constantly in a figure-eight motion with a wooden spoon. This ensures that the cheese melts smoothly into the wine.

Once the cheese is melted and velvety, stir in the kirsch and season with a pinch of nutmeg and a dash of freshly ground black pepper. Taste, adjust the seasoning, and reduce the heat to low, keeping the fondue warm and inviting.

Arrange the bread cubes and assorted vegetables around your cauldron of cheese. Invite your guests to spear their favorite morsels and dip them into the luscious cheese, relishing each gooey bite.

May your cauldron always bubble with joy and laughter, and may the enchantment of Witch's Brew Cheese Fondue linger long after the last morsel is devoured. Here's to magical moments and delicious memories that will haunt your taste buds long after the night is over!

12. Haunted Haystack Bites

As the autumn leaves fall and the cool breeze whispers tales of the supernatural, these Haunted Haystack Bites bring a bit of spooky fun to your Halloween festivities. They're the perfect eerie treat to make with your little ghosts and goblins, infusing your kitchen with bewitching aromas and giggles.

Preparation time: 10 minutes
Cooking time: 10 minutes
Ready-in time: 20 minutes
Serving size: 4 people

Ingredients:
2 cups chow mein noodles
1 cup butterscotch chips
1/2 cup creamy peanut butter
1/2 cup mini marshmallows
1/4 cup candy corn
1/4 cup Halloween-themed sprinkles

Instructions:

Now, my dear friends, let's embark on creating these delightful Halloween treats. Begin by gathering your ingredients, as this will make the whole process as smooth as a witch's ride on her broomstick. First, in a medium-sized microwave-safe bowl, combine the butterscotch chips and creamy peanut butter. Place the bowl in the microwave, and on medium power, gently melt the mixture in 30-second increments. Stir in between each interval until it's silky smooth and perfectly combined.

Next, stir in the chow mein noodles, ensuring each strand is luxuriously coated with the butterscotch-peanut butter concoction. This is where the magic happens, as the noodles transform into our haystack base. Add in the mini marshmallows, folding them in gently so they don't lose their pillowy charm.

Now, the fun part—the assembly. Using a spoon, drop small mounds of the mixture onto a parchment-lined baking sheet, forming spooky haystacks. Be sure to work quickly as the mixture can set faster than one might think. Once your haystacks are formed, press a few candy corn pieces into each one, providing a pop of color and a touch of whimsy. Sprinkle generously with Halloween-themed sprinkles for an extra dash of festive flair.

Allow your haunted haystacks to cool at room temperature until firm, about 10 minutes. Once set, they are ready to be devoured by eager trick-or-treaters.

These Haunted Haystack Bites serve as a delightful reminder of the enchanting power of food to bring together friends and family. Enjoy these bites of spooky joy, and may your Halloween be filled with laughter and delightful frights!

13. Graveyard Guacamole Cups

In the eerie glow of Halloween's haunting moon, one must conjure a dish that is both deliciously ghoulish and irresistibly fun. Gather your goblins and let's dive into a graveyard-inspired guacamole that promises to be the life—or death—of your spooky soirée.

Preparation time: 20 minutes
Cooking time: 0 minutes
Ready-in time: 20 minutes
Serving size: 4 people

Ingredients:
3 ripe avocados
1 lime, juiced
1 teaspoon salt
1 small onion, finely chopped
2 Roma tomatoes, diced
1 tablespoon chopped cilantro
1 clove garlic, minced
4 small corn tortillas
1 tablespoon olive oil
Black food coloring gel (optional)
4 pretzel sticks
8 candy eyes

Instructions:

First, let us embark on the guacamole journey. Begin by slicing the avocados in half, removing the pits, and scooping the luscious green flesh into a medium bowl. Add the fresh lime juice and sprinkle the salt generously. With a fork, mash the avocados to your desired consistency—some prefer a bit of chunk, others smooth as the night sky.

Next, stir in the finely chopped onion, the vibrant Roma tomatoes, the aromatic cilantro, and the subtle hint of minced garlic. Mix until all ingredients are evenly combined, ensuring each bite is a flavorful fiesta.

Now, for the gravestone chips. Preheat your oven to a toasty 350 degrees Fahrenheit. Take the small corn tortillas, and with a steady hand, cut them into tombstone shapes. Brush each with a whisper of olive oil, and if you're feeling extra spooky, add a touch of the black food coloring gel for an aged, haunted appearance.

Lay the tombstones on a baking sheet and bake until crisp and golden, about 10 minutes. Keep an eye on them, for we wouldn't want them to turn to ash!

To assemble, spoon the guacamole into four small cups. Artfully insert the tombstone chips into the guacamole, standing tall as if rising from the earth. Add two pretzel sticks to each cup, letting them peek out like eerie tree branches. Finish with a pair of candy eyes atop the guacamole for a delightful touch of whimsy.

Behold, your Graveyard Guacamole Cups are complete! A thrilling treat for young ghouls and wise witches alike. Share them with your coven, and watch as they vanish into the night, leaving only smiles behind. Until next time, remember to stir up a cauldron of creativity in your kitchen.

14. Zombie Zucchini Fritters

In a land where pumpkins reign supreme during the Halloween season, a humble zucchini decided to join the spooky festivities. These fritters are born from the magic of simple ingredients, transformed into ghoulishly delicious bites that even the pickiest of little monsters will adore.

Preparation time: 15 minutes
Cooking time: 20 minutes
Ready-in time: 35 minutes
Serving size: 4 people

Ingredients:
2 medium zucchinis, grated
1 teaspoon salt
1/4 cup all-purpose flour
1/4 cup grated Parmesan cheese
1 large egg, beaten
2 green onions, finely chopped
1 clove garlic, minced
1/2 teaspoon dried oregano
1/4 teaspoon black pepper
Vegetable oil, for frying
Sour cream or Greek yogurt, for serving

Instructions:

First, let's start by making our zucchini look like they've been through a frightful transformation. Grate your zucchinis into a large bowl and sprinkle them with salt. Allow this mixture to sit for about 10 minutes. This will help draw out excess water. Afterward, wrap the zucchini in a clean kitchen towel and squeeze out as much liquid as possible. We want our fritters to hold their shape and not be too watery.

In a mixing bowl, combine the drained zucchini with flour, Parmesan cheese, beaten egg, green onions, garlic, oregano, and pepper. Mix everything together until you have a cohesive batter that will hold its shape when scooped.

Now, heat a generous amount of vegetable oil in a large skillet over medium heat. You want just enough oil to cover the bottom of the pan. Once the oil is shimmering, drop spoonfuls of the zucchini batter into the pan, gently flattening them with the back of the spoon to create a fritter shape. Be sure not to overcrowd the pan, as we want each fritter to cook evenly and develop a delicious golden crust.

Cook each side for about 3-4 minutes or until golden brown and crispy. Once cooked, transfer the fritters to a paper towel-lined plate to drain any excess oil.

Serve these delightful zombie fritters warm, with a dollop of sour cream or Greek yogurt on top, and watch as they disappear faster than a ghost in a graveyard!

The zucchini may have started as a humble garden vegetable, but now it's the star of the Halloween party! These fritters are so frightfully good, they might just become a new family tradition. Enjoy every spooky bite and remember, even vegetables can join in on the Halloween fun!

15. Frightful Fruit Kabobs

When the moon casts eerie shadows, and little ghouls gather for a night of mischief, it's time to conjure up a treat that's both spooky and delightful. These Frightful Fruit Kabobs are sure to enchant even the most discerning goblins with their vibrant colors and playful presentation.

Preparation time: 20 minutes
Cooking time: None
Ready-in time: 20 minutes
Serving size: 4 people

Ingredients:
1 cup black grapes, washed
1 cup strawberries, hulled
1 cup cantaloupe, cubed
1 cup kiwi, peeled and sliced
4 wooden skewers
1 cup vanilla yogurt
2 tablespoons honey
1 teaspoon cinnamon
Handful of mini marshmallows

Instructions:

Start by creating a magical workspace with your ingredients laid out like a painter's palette. Each piece of fruit will be a brushstroke on our fruity canvas. Take your wooden skewers and begin the delightful process of threading. Begin with a plump black grape, followed by a juicy strawberry, then a cube of the sunny cantaloupe, and finish with a vibrant slice of kiwi. Repeat this sequence until your skewer is a delightful rainbow of spooky flavors.

Once your skewers are assembled, let's make a dipping potion. In a small bowl, stir together the creamy vanilla yogurt, sweet honey, and a dash of cinnamon. This concoction will serve as a delightful cauldron for your kabobs to be dipped into.

For an extra touch of whimsy, add a mini marshmallow atop each skewer, like a ghostly figure watching over your creation. Arrange these colorful kabobs on a platter, and place the yogurt dip in a charmingly eerie dish at the center for guests to enjoy.

Keep these in the refrigerator until it's time to serve, ensuring they remain as fresh as a cool autumn breeze.

Now, breathe in the enchantment as you serve these treats. Watch as they vanish as if by magic, leaving behind only smiles and a hint of mystery. Remember, the true magic of Halloween lies not in the treats themselves but in the joy they bring to young and old alike.

16. Sinister Salsa Skulls

In the spirit of Halloween, when the moon is high and shadows dance mischievously, we embark on a culinary adventure to create Sinister Salsa Skulls. These delightful edible creations are sure to thrill and chill, bringing a touch of the macabre to your festive celebration.

Preparation time: 15 minutes
Cooking time: 10 minutes
Ready-in time: 25 minutes
Serving size: 4 people

Ingredients:
4 mini bell peppers
1 cup fresh salsa
1 cup shredded cheddar cheese
4 large tortilla wraps
1 tablespoon olive oil
Salt and pepper to taste
1 teaspoon ground cumin
1 lime, cut into wedges
Fresh cilantro leaves for garnish

Instructions:

Begin by preheating your oven to 375°F (190°C). As it warms, slice the tops off the mini bell peppers and carefully remove the seeds, creating little hollow skulls. Next, take your tortilla wraps and cut out skull shapes using a knife or cookie cutter—aim for about the size of your palm, keeping them uniform.

Now, let's prepare the filling. In a mixing bowl, combine the fresh salsa, shredded cheddar cheese, a pinch of salt, pepper, and the ground cumin. Stir until everything melds into a vibrant, cheesy mixture that will soon fill our skulls with flavor.

Using a small spoon, carefully stuff each bell pepper with the salsa mixture, pressing in gently to ensure each one is generously filled. Place the stuffed peppers on a baking tray lined with parchment paper, and brush them lightly with olive oil.

Arrange your tortilla skulls on a separate baking tray, brushing them with olive oil as well, and sprinkle a dash of salt for extra flavor. Pop both trays into the oven—bake the peppers for about 10 minutes or until they are tender and the cheese is bubbling happily. The tortilla skulls will need just 5–7 minutes until they're golden and crisp.

Once everything is cooked to perfection, remove from the oven and let them cool slightly. Serve the sinister skulls with extra salsa on the side, a wedge of lime for a zesty squeeze, and a sprinkle of fresh cilantro to add a touch of green.

Voila! As the night unfolds, may these Sinister Salsa Skulls add a mischievous grin to your table. Remember, the real magic lies in sharing these eerie edibles with loved ones, amidst laughter and ghostly tales. Until our next spooky culinary adventure, bon appétit!

17. Jack-O'-Lantern Stuffed Peppers

As the autumn leaves fall and Halloween approaches, transform your kitchen into a whimsical wonderland with these delightful Jack-O'-Lantern Stuffed Peppers. Perfect for little hands to help, these charming treats are as fun to make as they are to eat, casting a spell of deliciousness at your table.

Preparation time: 20 minutes
Cooking time: 30 minutes
Ready-in time: 50 minutes
Serving size: 4 people

Ingredients:
4 large orange bell peppers
1 tablespoon olive oil
1 small onion, finely chopped
2 cloves garlic, minced
1 cup cooked rice
1 cup canned black beans, drained and rinsed
1 cup corn kernels, fresh or frozen
1 teaspoon ground cumin
1 teaspoon paprika
Salt and pepper to taste
1 cup shredded cheddar cheese
Fresh cilantro, chopped, for garnish

Instructions:

Begin by preheating your oven to a cozy 375°F (190°C). While the oven warms, take a sharp paring knife and carefully slice the tops off the bell peppers, setting aside these charming lids. Gently remove the seeds and membranes inside, creating a hollow space for our delectable filling.

Now, with an artistic touch, carve playful jack-o'-lantern faces into each pepper. Nothing too intricate—just simple triangles for eyes and a jagged smile will do. Set these charismatic peppers aside and turn your attention to the filling.

In a skillet over medium heat, warm the olive oil. Add the finely chopped onion and sauté until translucent, about 3 minutes. Stir in the garlic, allowing its fragrant aroma to fill the air for another minute. Next, fold in the cooked rice, black beans, and corn. Season this colorful mix with cumin, paprika, salt, and pepper, stirring until well combined.

Spoon this flavorful filling into each carved pepper, pressing gently to ensure they're generously stuffed. Sprinkle the tops with a blanket of cheddar cheese. Place the peppers in a baking dish, cover loosely with foil, and bake for about 25 minutes. Remove the foil, and let them bake for an additional 5 minutes, allowing the cheese to melt and bubble.

Once ready, remove from the oven and garnish with a sprinkle of fresh cilantro. Serve these bewitching Jack-O'-Lanterns warm, and watch as smiles light up like lanterns around your table.

And there you have it—an enchanting dish that turns Halloween into a feast for the eyes and the palate. These Jack-O'-Lantern Stuffed Peppers are sure to become a family favorite, as delightful to create as they are to devour. Happy Halloween, and may your celebrations be filled with joy and magic!

18. Terrifying Taco Cups

As the moon casts an eerie glow and little goblins gather for a night of fright, what better way to delight them than with a spooky twist on a classic favorite? These Terrifying Taco Cups are sure to enchant with their ghoulishly good flavors and playful presentation.

Preparation time: 15 minutes
Cooking time: 10 minutes
Ready-in time: 25 minutes
Serving size: 4 people

Ingredients:
12 wonton wrappers
1 cup cooked ground beef or turkey, seasoned with taco seasoning
1/2 cup shredded cheese (cheddar or Mexican blend)
1/2 cup black beans, drained and rinsed
1/2 cup salsa
1/4 cup sour cream
1/4 cup sliced black olives
1 avocado, diced
1 tablespoon chopped fresh cilantro
Salt and pepper, to taste

Instructions:

Let's begin by preheating our oven to 375°F (190°C), shall we? While the oven warms, take a muffin tin and gently tuck a wonton wrapper into each cup. They should look like little ghostly cloaks awaiting their filling.

Next, in a mixing bowl, combine your seasoned ground beef or turkey with the black beans and a few tablespoons of salsa. Spoon a generous tablespoon of this mixture into each wonton cup. Top it all with a sprinkle of shredded cheese — this will melt into gooey goodness.

Pop these frightful delights into the oven for about 10 minutes, until the wonton wrappers are crisp and golden, and the cheese is bubbling invitingly.

Once out of the oven, let them cool slightly before adding a dollop of sour cream on top of each taco cup. For a touch of eerie elegance, scatter some sliced black olives and fresh cilantro over the top. Finish with a few cubes of avocado, adding a creamy texture to each bite.

Season with a pinch of salt and pepper, then serve your Terrifying Taco Cups while they're still warm. They're sure to vanish as quickly as a ghost in the night!

And there you have it, a delightful fright to thrill your guests! May these taco cups bring as much joy as they do screams of delight this Halloween. Remember, creativity in the kitchen can be as enchanting as any spell. Happy haunting!

19. Batty Bruschetta

As the moonlight casts eerie shadows, conjure a plate of Batty Bruschetta to delight your little ghosts and goblins. This whimsical twist on a classic favorite will have everyone howling with delight and reaching for more. Little bats, beware—your savory secret is about to be unveiled!

Preparation time: 15 minutes
Cooking time: 10 minutes
Ready-in time: 25 minutes
Serving size: 4 people

Ingredients:
1 baguette, sliced into 12 pieces
3 tablespoons olive oil
2 cloves garlic, peeled and halved
2 medium tomatoes, finely diced
1/4 cup fresh basil leaves, julienned
Salt and pepper, to taste
1/2 cup mozzarella cheese, shredded
12 black olives, pitted and halved
Balsamic glaze, for drizzling

Instructions:

Begin by preheating your oven to a toasty 400°F (200°C). While the oven is warming, lay your baguette slices on a baking sheet, brushing each with a whisper of olive oil. Into the oven, they go for about 5 minutes, until golden and crispy—like sun-kissed autumn leaves.

Once they're toasted to perfection, run a garlic clove gently across each slice, infusing them with a hint of aromatic allure. In a small mixing bowl, combine the diced tomatoes with fresh basil, seasoning with a touch of salt and a sprinkle of pepper. Let this mixture rest, melding flavors in a delightful dance.

Top each garlic-rubbed toast with a generous spoonful of your tomato-basil concoction. Next, scatter a gentle snowfall of mozzarella cheese across them, before placing two olive halves on each slice—these will form the body of our little bats.

Return the bruschetta to the oven for another 5 minutes, just enough for the cheese to melt into a creamy dream. Once out, drizzle a whimsical trail of balsamic glaze over each piece.

Serve immediately, and watch as these charming batty bites disappear into the night.

With a swoop and a flutter, these Batty Bruschetta will vanish faster than you can say 'Trick or Treat.' A spine-tingling success for your Halloween gathering, they're bound to bewitch both young and old alike. Happy haunting, and enjoy every bite!

20. Pumpkin Patch Cheese Spread

As the autumn leaves start to waltz in the crisp breeze and pumpkins adorn every doorstep, what better way to celebrate the season than with a delightful cheese spread? This whimsical recipe will transform your table into a festive pumpkin patch that even the littlest ghouls will adore.

Preparation time: 15 minutes
Cooking time: 5 minutes
Ready-in time: 20 minutes
Serving size: 4 people

Ingredients:
8 ounces cream cheese, softened
1 cup shredded sharp cheddar cheese
1/4 cup sour cream
1/4 cup canned pumpkin puree
1 tablespoon honey
1/2 teaspoon ground cinnamon
1/4 teaspoon nutmeg
Salt and pepper to taste
2 green onions, thinly sliced
Crackers or sliced vegetables for serving

Instructions:

Begin by gathering your ingredients and letting the cream cheese soften to room temperature. In a large mixing bowl, combine the cream cheese, shredded cheddar cheese, sour cream, and pumpkin puree. With an electric mixer, blend until smooth and creamy, making sure each ingredient melds into a well-mixed harmony.

Next, add the honey, ground cinnamon, and nutmeg, then sprinkle in a dash of salt and pepper to suit your taste. Stir gently to infuse the spread with a hint of autumnal warmth. Once it's well combined, fold in the green onions, reserving a few slices for a decorative garnish.

Transfer this delightful spread into a serving bowl and shape it into a charming little pumpkin. For an artistic touch, use your knife to gently score lines down the sides, mimicking the natural grooves of a pumpkin. Top your creation with a few green onion slices, artfully arranged to resemble the vine-like tendrils of a pumpkin patch.

Serve your Pumpkin Patch Cheese Spread with an array of crackers or crisp vegetable slices. Watch as your guests become entranced by this enchanting and savory delight, perfect for any Halloween gathering.

Ah, there you have it! A magical spread that captures the essence of fall and the playful spirit of Halloween. Whether enjoyed by little ones or the young at heart, this cheese spread will surely become a seasonal favorite. Bon appétit!

21. Monster Mac & Cheese

In the mystical realm of culinary delight, imagine a bubbling cauldron of cheesy goodness, where mac and cheese are transformed into a monstrous feast! This spooky spin on a beloved classic will delight young ghouls and goblins, casting a spell of deliciousness at your Halloween gathering.

Preparation time: 15 minutes
Cooking time: 30 minutes
Ready-in time: 45 minutes
Serving size: 4 people

Ingredients:
8 ounces elbow macaroni
2 tablespoons unsalted butter
2 tablespoons all-purpose flour
2 cups whole milk
1 ½ cups shredded sharp cheddar cheese
½ cup shredded mozzarella cheese
A pinch of nutmeg
Salt and pepper, to taste
Green food coloring
4 pretzel sticks
4 black olives
4 cherry tomatoes
4 slices of pepperoni

Instructions:

First, let's boil the macaroni. Bring a large pot of salted water to a rolling boil, then add the pasta, cooking until al dente, about 8 minutes. Drain well and set aside. Now, in a medium saucepan over medium heat, melt the butter. Once melted, sprinkle in the flour, whisking continuously for about a minute to create a smooth roux.

Gradually pour in the milk, whisking constantly until the mixture thickens and starts to bubble gently. Now, it's time to melt in the magic. Stir in the cheddar and mozzarella cheeses, letting them blend into a creamy sauce. Add a whisper of nutmeg, and season with salt and pepper to taste.

Here comes the spooky twist: add a few drops of green food coloring to the cheese sauce until it reaches a monstrous hue. Combine the cooked macaroni with the vibrant cheese sauce, stirring until everything is deliciously coated.

To fashion your creature's face, spoon the mac and cheese into bowls. For eyes, use black olives perched on pretzel sticks. Cherry tomatoes make perfect noses, and pepperoni slices craft ghoulish mouths.

And there you have it, a Monster Mac & Cheese that's frightfully fun and fabulously flavorful!

Remember, nothing brings a family together quite like a monstrously good meal. So gather around, giggle at your creations, and savor every spooky bite. Until next time, may your kitchen be as enchanting as a witch's brew!

22. Jack-O'-Lantern Pizzas

As the autumn leaves crunch underfoot and spirited whispers fill the air, it's time to conjure up mischievous smiles with delightful Jack-O'-Lantern Pizzas. These charming creations are as fun to make as they are to devour—perfect for an afternoon of family frolics in the kitchen.

Preparation time: 15 minutes
Cooking time: 15 minutes
Ready-in time: 30 minutes
Serving size: 4 people

Ingredients:
4 small whole wheat pita breads
1 cup pizza sauce
1 ½ cups shredded mozzarella cheese
1 cup sliced pepperoni
1 green bell pepper
Black olives for decoration
Olive oil for brushing
Salt and pepper to taste

Instructions:

Begin by gathering your eager little chefs and preheating the oven to a warm 400°F (200°C). Place the pita breads on a baking sheet lined with parchment paper, and lightly brush each with a touch of olive oil. This will ensure a crispy, golden crust that makes our Jack-O'-Lantern Pizzas simply irresistible.

Now, spread a generous spoonful of pizza sauce over each pita, leaving a small border around the edges. The sauce is the heart of our pizzas, providing a rich, tangy base that brings everything together.

Next, sprinkle the shredded mozzarella cheese over each pita, creating a snow-dusted landscape for our jack-o'-lantern faces to shine. Be liberal with the cheese, as it melts into gooey perfection, binding our toppings in delicious harmony.

For the faces, use slices of pepperoni to form mischievous grins and triangular eyes. Cut the green bell pepper into thin strips to fashion stems and eyebrows, adding a pop of color to our edible lanterns. Finally, place a few black olives as pupils or noses to bring the faces to life.

Slide the baking sheet into the oven and let the magic happen for about 15 minutes, or until the cheese is bubbling joyfully and the edges are golden brown.

Remove your creations from the oven and let them cool for a moment. Then, gather the family around and enjoy these whimsical Jack-O'-Lantern Pizzas, crafted with care and a pinch of Halloween spirit.

The delight of creating these pizzas is only matched by the joy of seeing them devoured. Nothing warms the heart more than the laughter shared over a meal made together. Until our next culinary adventure, may your days be filled with warmth and creativity!

23. Zombie Meatloaf

As the moonlight spills through your kitchen window and shadows dance across the walls, summon your inner culinary wizard to craft a dish that will delight and surprise. This zombie meatloaf is a macabre masterpiece, perfect for a frightfully fun Halloween gathering with family and friends.

Preparation time: 25 minutes
Cooking time: 1 hour
Ready-in time: 1 hour 25 minutes
Serving size: 4 people

Ingredients:
1 pound ground beef
1/2 pound ground pork
1/2 cup breadcrumbs
1/4 cup milk
1/4 cup ketchup
1 tablespoon Worcestershire sauce
1 teaspoon garlic powder
1 teaspoon onion powder
1/2 teaspoon salt
1/2 teaspoon black pepper
1 egg
1 small onion, finely chopped
2 mozzarella cheese sticks
1 small red bell pepper
1/4 cup black olives
1/4 cup ketchup for glaze

Instructions:

Let's begin by setting the stage for our ghoulish creation. Preheat your oven to 350°F (175°C). In a large mixing bowl, combine the ground beef and pork, breadcrumbs, milk, ketchup, Worcestershire sauce, garlic powder, onion powder, salt, pepper, and the egg. Add the finely chopped onion, and with clean hands, gently mix everything together until well combined but not overworked. We want a tender zombie loaf, after all.

Next, line a baking sheet with parchment paper. Shape the meat mixture into a slightly oval mound—this is the zombie's head. Now, let's give our zombie some character. Insert the mozzarella cheese sticks partially into the meatloaf to create bulging eyes. Slice the red bell pepper into strips and arrange them to mimic a creepy, crooked smile.

Cover the meatloaf with a glaze of ketchup, spreading it evenly for that perfect undead hue. Pop it into the preheated oven and let it cook for about an hour, or until it's thoroughly cooked through. As it bakes, slice the black olives into rounds to use later as pupils.

Once the timer chimes, remove the meatloaf and let it rest for a few minutes. Use the black olive slices to complete the eyes, placing one in the center of each cheese stick. Your zombie meatloaf is now ready to lurch onto the dining table!

As you slice into this eerie delight, watch the delight spark in your little monsters' eyes. Remember, Halloween is about fun and imagination—so let your creativity run wild, and may your culinary adventures be ever deliciously spooky. Happy Halloween!

24. Witch's Cauldron Chili

In the moonlit glow of Halloween night, a simmering cauldron of chili can transform a humble kitchen into a spellbinding feast for young witches and wizards. Bewitched with a concoction of flavors, this chili promises to be a delightfully eerie addition to your festive table.

Preparation time: 20 minutes
Cooking time: 1 hour
Ready-in time: 1 hour 20 minutes
Serving size: 4 people

Ingredients:
2 tablespoons olive oil
1 medium onion, finely chopped
3 cloves garlic, minced
1 pound ground beef
1 can (15 ounces) black beans, drained and rinsed
1 can (15 ounces) kidney beans, drained and rinsed
1 can (14.5 ounces) diced tomatoes
2 tablespoons tomato paste
1 cup beef broth
2 teaspoons chili powder
1 teaspoon ground cumin
1 teaspoon smoked paprika
Salt and pepper to taste
1 bell pepper, chopped
1 cup corn kernels, fresh or frozen
1 tablespoon apple cider vinegar
1 cup shredded cheddar cheese, for serving
Sour cream, for serving
Chopped green onions, for garnish

Instructions:

Begin by heating the olive oil in a large pot over medium heat. Add the finely chopped onion and minced garlic, allowing them to sauté until the onion turns translucent and fragrant, about 5 minutes. Introduce the ground beef, breaking it apart with a wooden spoon. Cook until it's browned and no pink remains.

Now, it's time to add a little magic to your pot. Stir in the black beans, kidney beans, diced tomatoes, and tomato paste. Pour in the beef broth, and then sprinkle in the chili powder, cumin, and smoked paprika. Season with salt and pepper, stirring everything together until well combined.

Incorporate the bell pepper and corn kernels into the mix, stirring gently. Reduce the heat to low, cover the pot, and let it simmer for about 45 minutes. This gives the flavors a chance to meld beautifully.

Just before serving, stir in the apple cider vinegar, adding a subtle tang that elevates the dish to enchanting heights. Ladle the chili into bowls, and top generously with shredded cheddar cheese, a dollop of sour cream, and a sprinkle of green onions.

Take a moment to enjoy the symphony of flavors dancing in your bowl. This Witch's Cauldron Chili is sure to cast a delicious spell over your family and friends. Remember, the best magic is always shared with those you love. Happy Halloween!

25. Frightening Fajitas

As the autumn leaves dance whimsically in the crisp evening breeze, why not invite a little culinary spookiness into your kitchen? These Frightening Fajitas promise to captivate both young trick-or-treaters and seasoned gourmands alike, ensuring your Halloween feast is us delightfully eerie as it is delicious.

Preparation time: 15 minutes
Cooking time: 20 minutes
Ready-in time: 35 minutes
Serving size: 4 people

Ingredients:
1 pound boneless, skinless chicken breasts, sliced into thin strips
1 red bell pepper, thinly sliced
1 green bell pepper, thinly sliced
1 medium red onion, thinly sliced
2 tablespoons olive oil
2 teaspoons smoked paprika
1 teaspoon garlic powder
1 teaspoon onion powder
1 teaspoon ground cumin
1 teaspoon chili powder
Salt and pepper, to taste
8 small flour tortillas
1 cup shredded cheddar cheese
1 cup guacamole
1 cup sour cream
1 cup salsa
Lime wedges, for garnish
Fresh cilantro leaves, for garnish

Instructions:

First, gather your ingredients as if assembling a magical potion. In a large mixing bowl, combine the chicken strips with olive oil, smoked paprika, garlic powder, onion powder, ground cumin, chili powder, salt, and pepper. Toss everything together until the chicken is thoroughly coated with this enchanting blend of spices.

Now, heat a large skillet over medium-high heat. Add a touch more olive oil if needed, and once shimmering, introduce the chicken to the pan. Cook, stirring occasionally, until the chicken is golden and cooked through—approximately 6 to 8 minutes should suffice. Remove the chicken from the skillet and set it aside, keeping it warm in a cozy foil wrap.

In the same skillet, add the sliced bell peppers and onion. Sauté these colorful companions until they're softened and slightly charred, about 7 minutes. Return the chicken to the skillet, stirring everything together in a harmonious medley of flavors.

Warm the flour tortillas in a dry skillet or microwave. To assemble your frightening fajitas, lay a tortilla flat and spoon a generous portion of the chicken and vegetable mixture onto it. Sprinkle with shredded cheddar cheese, and add a dollop of guacamole and sour cream. Top with a spoonful of salsa, a squeeze of lime, and a sprinkle of fresh cilantro.

Roll up your fajita, and repeat with the remaining tortillas. Serve with extra lime wedges and a side of your favorite Halloween tales.

With each bite of these Frightening Fajitas, you'll find yourself weaving stories of culinary magic. Let the flavors transport you to a realm where every meal becomes an unforgettable adventure. Here's to delightful frights and tantalizing bites!

26. Spooky Spaghetti and Eyeballs

As twilight descends and the little goblins begin their annual haunting, it's time to transform your dining table into a realm of delightful fright. This Spooky Spaghetti and Eyeballs dish will charm and thrill, making your Halloween feast a deliciously memorable event for all ages.

Preparation time: 15 minutes
Cooking time: 30 minutes
Ready-in time: 45 minutes
Serving size: 4 people

Ingredients:
12 ounces spaghetti
2 tablespoons olive oil
1 small onion, finely chopped
2 cloves garlic, minced
1 can (15 ounces) tomato sauce
1 teaspoon dried oregano
Salt and pepper to taste
1 pound ground beef
1/4 cup breadcrumbs
1/4 cup grated Parmesan cheese
1 large egg
16 small mozzarella balls
16 small pimento-stuffed olives

Instructions:

Begin by cooking the spaghetti according to package instructions in a large pot of boiling salted water until al dente. Drain well and set aside. Now, in a medium skillet, heat the olive oil over medium heat. Sauté the onion and garlic until they become translucent and aromatic, about 3 minutes.

Next, pour in the tomato sauce and add the oregano, stirring to combine. Season with salt and pepper, then reduce the heat to low and let it simmer gently while we prepare the meatballs.

In a large mixing bowl, combine the ground beef, breadcrumbs, Parmesan, and egg. Use your hands to mix until everything is well incorporated. Shape the mixture into 16 small meatballs.

Heat a large skillet over medium heat and cook the meatballs until they are browned on all sides and cooked through, about 8-10 minutes. Remove from the heat and let them cool slightly.

Here comes the fun part! For each eyeball, take a mozzarella ball and press a pimento-stuffed olive into the center. Top each meatball with one of these spooky eyeballs.

To serve, place a generous portion of spaghetti on each plate, ladle over the rich tomato sauce, and arrange the eyeball-topped meatballs on top. Watch the delighted screams and giggles unfold!

Gather 'round, for you have conjured a dish that inspires both fright and delight! As your family enjoys this eerie creation, may your evening be filled with laughter, love, and a touch of mystery. Bon appétit, dear friends, on this bewitchingly wonderful night!

27. Mummy Meatball Subs

 # 27. Mummy Meatball Subs

On a crisp autumn evening, what could be more delightful than crafting a culinary creature that will amuse and satisfy the whole family? These Mummy Meatball Subs, wrapped with care and a touch of whimsy, promise to be the highlight of your Halloween festivities, leaving both young and old spellbound.

Preparation time: 20 minutes
Cooking time: 25 minutes
Ready-in time: 45 minutes
Serving size: 4 people

Ingredients:
1 pound ground beef
1/2 cup breadcrumbs
1/4 cup grated Parmesan cheese
1 egg
2 cloves garlic, minced
1/2 teaspoon salt
1/4 teaspoon black pepper
1 teaspoon Italian seasoning
1 cup marinara sauce
4 submarine rolls
8 slices mozzarella cheese
1 can (8 ounces) refrigerated crescent roll dough
Black olives, sliced, for eyes
Cooking spray

Instructions:

First, let's preheat our oven to 375 degrees Fahrenheit—setting the stage for our spooky creation. In a large bowl, combine the ground beef with breadcrumbs, Parmesan, egg, garlic, salt, pepper, and Italian seasoning. Mix gently yet thoroughly with your hands until everything is well incorporated. Now, shape this savory mixture into delightful 1-inch meatballs, placing them on a baking sheet lightly coated with cooking spray.

Let's bake these meatballs for about 15 minutes until they're browned and cooked through. While they sizzle away, warm the marinara sauce over medium heat in a saucepan, letting those flavors meld beautifully.

As the meatballs finish, slice the submarine rolls in half, placing two slices of mozzarella cheese on each bottom half. Nestle about 3 to 4 meatballs gently atop the cheese, spooning that rich marinara sauce lovingly over them.

Now, for the fun part—turning these subs into mummies! Unroll the crescent dough and cut into thin strips, wrapping them playfully around each sub to mimic bandages. Leave small gaps here and there to peek through. Return them to the oven for an additional 10 minutes, or until the dough is golden and cheese is delightfully melty.

Finally, place two olive slices for eyes on each mummy sub, bringing them to life with a touch of whimsy.

Gather everyone around and watch their surprised delight as these charming mummies appear from the kitchen. With each bite, you're sure to hear giggles and perhaps a ghostly 'boo!' Enjoy the magic of the season with every deliciously wrapped sub.

28. Creepy-Crawly Casserole

As the autumn leaves crunch beneath our feet and shadows lengthen, there's no better time to indulge in a little culinary mischief. With this Creepy-Crawly Casserole, you'll enchant your family with delightful spookiness that's sure to become a Halloween tradition.

Preparation time: 20 minutes
Cooking time: 30 minutes
Ready-in time: 50 minutes
Serving size: 4 people

Ingredients:
1 pound ground turkey
1 tablespoon olive oil
1 small onion, finely chopped
2 cloves garlic, minced
1 red bell pepper, diced
1 can (14.5 ounces) diced tomatoes, undrained
1 teaspoon smoked paprika
1/2 teaspoon ground cumin
Salt and pepper to taste
1 cup cooked quinoa
1 cup shredded mozzarella cheese
1/2 cup black olives, sliced
1/4 cup fresh cilantro, chopped
1 bag tortilla chips, for garnish
Candy eyes (found at craft stores), for decoration

Instructions:

First, let's bring a little magic into the kitchen. Begin by heating olive oil in a large skillet over medium heat. Add the finely chopped onion and garlic, allowing them to soften and release their enchanting aroma. Stir in the ground turkey, breaking it apart with a wooden spoon, until it's beautifully browned.

Next, add the red bell pepper, diced tomatoes, smoked paprika, and cumin. Give it a good stir, and let it simmer gently, as the flavors mingle and dance together. Season with salt and pepper to your liking.

Once your bubbling potion is ready, stir in the cooked quinoa and half of the mozzarella cheese, letting everything melt into delicious harmony.

Transfer this delightful mixture into a baking dish, spreading it evenly. Sprinkle the remaining mozzarella cheese on top, creating a layer of gooey goodness. Arrange the black olives like little creepy-crawly bugs crawling across the surface.

Place the casserole in a preheated oven at 375°F (190°C) and let it bake for about 20 minutes, until the cheese is melted and golden.

Remove from the oven, and sprinkle fresh cilantro over the top, adding a splash of vibrant green. Scatter tortilla chips around the edges, resembling a nest for your creepy-crawlies. Finally, add candy eyes to the olives for a playful touch.

And there you have it, a Creepy-Crawly Casserole ready to delight and spook in equal measure.

Gather around the table, and let this eerie feast cast a spell of laughter and delight on your Halloween festivities. Remember, it's not just about the food; it's about creating memories that last a lifetime. Enjoy every bite of this spooky surprise!

29. Haunted Hot Dogs

As the moon casts eerie shadows and the crisp autumn air whispers tales of the supernatural, gather around for a spooky treat that's as fun to make as it is to eat. These Haunted Hot Dogs will delight kids and adults alike with their ghostly appearance and delicious flavors.

Preparation time: 15 minutes
Cooking time: 10 minutes
Ready-in time: 25 minutes
Serving size: 4 people

Ingredients:
8 hot dogs
1 sheet of puff pastry, thawed
1 egg, beaten
2 tablespoons ketchup
2 tablespoons mustard
8 black olives, sliced into rounds

Instructions:

Begin by preheating your oven to 375 degrees Fahrenheit. As the oven warms, let's get our hands busy with the hot dogs. Take each hot dog and slice it in half lengthwise, then set them aside. Now, unroll your puff pastry onto a lightly floured surface. With a sharp knife or pizza cutter, slice the pastry into thin strips, about half an inch wide.

Wrap each half of the hot dog with a strip of puff pastry, leaving a small gap at the top for the face of our little haunted friends. Be certain to secure the ends of the pastry by gently pressing them down. Once all the hot dogs are snug in their pastry blankets, place them on a parchment-lined baking sheet.

Brush each wrapped hot dog with the beaten egg. This step is crucial as it gives them that lovely golden hue. Now, pop them into the oven and let them bake for about 10 minutes, or until the pastry is puffed and golden.

While they bake, prepare your ghostly faces. Dab a small amount of ketchup or mustard on each olive slice to act as glue, and place them onto the exposed hot dog peeking through the pastry. Once out of the oven, allow them to cool slightly before serving with additional ketchup and mustard for dipping.

Gather your little goblins and witches, for the feast of the Haunted Hot Dogs is ready! Watch their eyes widen with glee as the spooky snacks disappear, one by one, into delighted tummies. Happy haunting, and may your Halloween be filled with laughter and delicious frights!

30. Vampire's Veggie Stir Fry

As darkness falls and the moon casts its eerie glow, what better dish to serve than a Vampire's Veggie Stir Fry? Imagine a cauldron of vibrant colors and intriguing flavors, a feast for both the eyes and the taste buds, ready to delight your little ghouls and goblins.

Preparation time: 15 minutes
Cooking time: 10 minutes
Ready-in time: 25 minutes
Serving size: 4 people

Ingredients:
2 tablespoons olive oil
3 cloves garlic, finely minced
1-inch piece of fresh ginger, grated
1 red bell pepper, sliced
1 yellow bell pepper, sliced
1 cup broccoli florets
1 cup sugar snap peas
1 cup sliced mushrooms
1/2 cup baby corn, halved
2 tablespoons soy sauce
1 tablespoon hoisin sauce
1 teaspoon sesame oil
Salt and pepper to taste
1 tablespoon sesame seeds
2 green onions, thinly sliced
1 cup cooked jasmine rice

Instructions:

Begin by heating your olive oil in a large skillet or wok over medium-high heat. As the oil shimmers, toss in the minced garlic and grated ginger. Allow them to sizzle and perfume the air with their tantalizing aroma for about 30 seconds. Now, add the vibrant red and yellow bell peppers, stirring them with a gentle hand to ensure they coat in the aromatic oil.

Next, introduce the broccoli florets, sugar snap peas, and sliced mushrooms into the pan. Let these vegetables mingle and soften slightly in the heat, about 3 to 4 minutes, stirring occasionally. Add the baby corn for a touch of sweetness, stirring for another minute.

Pour in the soy sauce, hoisin sauce, and sesame oil, stirring well to ensure each vegetable is draped in this delicious cloak of flavor. Season with a pinch of salt and pepper, adjusting to your taste preference. Allow everything to cook for another 2 minutes until the vegetables are tender yet still crisp.

Scatter the sesame seeds and green onions over your vibrant creation, giving everything a final stir. Serve this delightful stir fry over a bed of warm jasmine rice, letting the colors and textures shine.

Even the most daring of vampires would be tempted by this vibrant dish, a tribute to flavors that come alive under the moonlight. May your Halloween be filled with laughter, joy, and just the right amount of delightful spookiness!

31. Ghostly Grilled Cheese

In the enchanted world of culinary delight, where flavor meets fantasy, let's conjure up a spectral twist on a classic favorite. These Ghostly Grilled Cheese sandwiches will delight young ghouls and goblins alike, making your Halloween gathering both spooky and scrumptious.

Preparation time: 10 minutes
Cooking time: 6 minutes
Ready-in time: 16 minutes
Serving size: 4 people

Ingredients:
8 slices of white bread
4 tablespoons unsalted butter, softened
8 slices of mozzarella cheese
1 teaspoon garlic powder
1 teaspoon dried oregano
Black olive slices, for decoration
Ketchup, for drawing ghostly faces

Instructions:

Let's start by laying out the slices of bread on a clean surface. Gently spread softened butter on one side of each slice. This will ensure a golden, crispy exterior. Now, sprinkle a whisper of garlic powder and a hint of oregano on the buttered side to infuse each bite with enchanting flavors.

Next, place a delightful slice of mozzarella cheese onto the unbuttered side of half of the bread slices. Remember, this cheese is what will make our ghosts come to life. Top each cheese-laden slice with another piece of bread, buttered side facing outwards, creating a perfect sandwich.

In a non-stick skillet over medium heat, gently place your sandwiches. Allow them to cook for about 3 minutes on each side, until the bread transforms into a beautiful golden hue, and the cheese melts to a gooey delight. Patience is key here; let the magic happen.

As your sandwiches cool slightly, fashion them into ghostly shapes using a ghost-shaped cookie cutter. Now, it's time to give your ghostly creations a face. Using small black olive slices, form eyes, and with a little bit of ketchup, draw a hauntingly happy or spooky mouth.

Serve these spectral delights immediately, and watch as they disappear before your eyes!

Ah, the delight of sharing a dish that not only fills the tummy but also brings a smile to the face is truly magical. Let these ghostly grilled cheeses float into your Halloween celebrations, leaving a trail of joy and delicious memories. Until next time, may your kitchen be forever enchanting!

32. Skeleton Sliders

In the spirit of Halloween, let us summon a dish that delights, not frightens. These Skeleton Sliders are a whimsical treat that will have your little ghouls coming back for more. Crafted with creativity and a touch of spookiness, they transform a simple meal into a hauntingly fun experience.

Preparation time: 20 minutes
Cooking time: 10 minutes
Ready-in time: 30 minutes
Serving size: 4 people

Ingredients:
1 pound ground beef
1 teaspoon salt
1/2 teaspoon black pepper
1 tablespoon Worcestershire sauce
4 slices cheddar cheese
4 mini slider buns
1/4 cup mayonnaise
1 teaspoon Dijon mustard
4 large green olives, pitted and halved
8 small pretzel sticks
Lettuce leaves, for garnish
Ketchup, for decoration

Instructions:

First, gather your ingredients like a culinary wizard assembling a potion. Begin by mixing the ground beef, salt, black pepper, and Worcestershire sauce in a bowl. Form this mixture into 4 delightful patties, ensuring they are just slightly larger than your mini slider buns.

Heat a skillet over medium-high heat, and place your patties onto the sizzling surface. Cook each side for about 3-4 minutes until they are golden brown and cooked through. During the last minute of cooking, lay a slice of cheddar cheese over each patty, letting it melt into a gooey, delicious cloak.

Meanwhile, in a separate small bowl, whisk together the mayonnaise and Dijon mustard. Slice your slider buns in half and spread this creamy mixture on the insides.

Now, it's time to assemble. Place a lettuce leaf on the bottom half of each bun, crown it with a cheesy patty, and gently close the slider with the top bun. Insert a pretzel stick into each olive half, creating eerie eyes, and set them atop the sliders, securing them into place.

For an extra spooky touch, use a small amount of ketchup to draw skeleton-like details, perhaps a grin or two, on the cheese.

And voilà, your Skeleton Sliders are ready to haunt the dinner table!

With these sliders, let your Halloween festivities take a deliciously spooky turn, where every bite is a playful dance between the eerie and the delightful. May your gathering be filled with laughter and culinary enchantment, making memories that are both creepy and cherished!

33. Pumpkin Patch Pasta

When the autumn winds whistle and the leaves begin their whispered descent, there's nothing quite like a playful dish to warm both the heart and home. Gather the family, don your aprons, and prepare to conjure a delectable pasta that blends the whimsy of pumpkin patches with a dash of culinary magic.

Preparation time: 15 minutes
Cooking time: 20 minutes
Ready-in time: 35 minutes
Serving size: 4 people

Ingredients:
12 ounces fusilli pasta
1 tablespoon olive oil
1 small onion, finely chopped
2 cloves garlic, minced
1 cup pumpkin puree
1 cup heavy cream
1/2 teaspoon ground nutmeg
1/2 teaspoon cinnamon
Salt and freshly ground black pepper, to taste
1/4 cup grated Parmesan cheese
1/4 cup toasted pumpkin seeds
Fresh sage leaves, for garnish

Instructions:

Let's embark on this delightful culinary journey by first setting a pot of water to a rolling boil. Toss in the fusilli pasta, and let it cook until al dente, about 10 minutes. Meanwhile, in a cozy saucepan, gently heat the olive oil over medium heat. Add the finely chopped onion, stirring until it becomes translucent and fragrant, which should take about 5 minutes. Now, introduce the minced garlic, allowing it to mingle with the onion for just a minute.

With a wooden spoon, swirl in the pumpkin puree and heavy cream, watching as the mixture transforms into a creamy, orange-hued delight. Sprinkle in the nutmeg and cinnamon, seasoning with salt and pepper to your heart's content. Allow the sauce to simmer gently for about 5 minutes, stirring occasionally, until it thickens slightly.

Drain the pasta, reserving a ladleful of its cooking water. Introduce the pasta to the pumpkin sauce, adding a splash of the reserved water if the sauce needs a bit more fluidity. Sprinkle in the Parmesan cheese, letting it melt into the sauce, creating a harmonious blend.

To serve, dish the pasta onto plates, adorning each with a sprinkle of toasted pumpkin seeds and a few fresh sage leaves. This captivating dish is now ready to enchant your taste buds.

"Ah, the joy of sharing a meal that mirrors the colors of fall! As you savor this Pumpkin Patch Pasta, perhaps you'll find yourself dreaming of magical pumpkin patches or the sound of leaves crunching underfoot. Until our next culinary adventure, may your table always be a place of warmth and wonder.

34. Wicked Witch's Stew

On a moonlit night, when the shadows dance and the winds whisper secrets, gather your little goblins and prepare this enchanting stew. With a hint of magic and a dash of mystery, you'll soon have a cauldron bubbling over with flavors fit for a witch's feast.

Preparation time: 20 minutes
Cooking time: 45 minutes
Ready-in time: 1 hour 5 minutes
Serving size: 4 people

Ingredients:
2 tablespoons olive oil
1 medium onion, finely chopped
2 cloves garlic, minced
1 pound lean ground beef
2 carrots, sliced into thin rounds
2 stalks celery, chopped
1 zucchini, diced
1 can (14.5 ounces) diced tomatoes
4 cups beef broth
1 teaspoon dried thyme
1 teaspoon dried oregano
Salt and pepper to taste
1 cup small pasta shells
1 cup frozen peas
1 cup baby spinach leaves
1 tablespoon fresh parsley, chopped

Instructions:

Now, gather around and let's embark on this culinary adventure. Begin by heating the olive oil in a large pot over medium heat. As the oil shimmers, invite the onion and garlic to join the party, and sauté until they release their aromatic charm. Next, introduce the ground beef, cooking until it's browned and crumbled. Don't forget to whisper a little encouragement as you go.

Into the pot go the carrots, celery, and zucchini, allowing them to mingle with the beefy goodness. Pour in the diced tomatoes and beef broth, stirring with a wooden spoon to bring all the flavors together. Sprinkle in the thyme and oregano, adding salt and pepper to suit your taste.

Let this magical concoction simmer for about 20 minutes, then sprinkle the pasta shells into the bubbling brew. As the pasta approaches al dente perfection, toss in the frozen peas and baby spinach, giving them just enough time to blend into the hearty mix.

Finally, sprinkle the fresh parsley over the top, stirring it through the stew. As the aroma fills your kitchen, you'll know your Wicked Witch's Stew is ready to serve.

Gather round, dear ones, and let the warmth of this stew cast a spell of coziness over your evening. With each spoonful, may you find a hint of magic and a sprinkle of delight. Enjoy this enchanting creation, and may your Halloween be as flavorful as your feast!

35. Graveyard Goulash

In the spirit of Halloween, let's conjure a dish that's as spooky as it is scrumptious. This Graveyard Goulash is sure to bring a playful chill to your table, complete with edible tombstones and a hearty filling that will delight ghosts and goblins alike.

Preparation time: 20 minutes
Cooking time: 40 minutes
Ready-in time: 1 hour
Serving size: 4 people

Ingredients:
1 pound ground beef
1 large onion, finely chopped
2 cloves garlic, minced
1 red bell pepper, diced
1 can (14.5 ounces) diced tomatoes
1 can (6 ounces) tomato paste
1 teaspoon paprika
1 teaspoon dried oregano
Salt and pepper, to taste
1 cup beef broth
8 ounces egg noodles
1/2 cup sour cream
4 slices of bread, cut into tombstone shapes
1 tablespoon butter, melted

Instructions:

Now, let's begin our culinary journey into the graveyard. In a large skillet over medium heat, brown the ground beef until it's cooked through, occasionally stirring to avoid any haunting surprises. Drain any excess fat, as we want our goulash light and lively. Add the chopped onion and minced garlic, letting them mingle with the beef until they're fragrant and translucent—about five minutes should do the trick.

Next, toss in the diced red bell pepper, canned tomatoes, and tomato paste. Stir in the paprika, oregano, and a pinch of salt and pepper. Allow this mixture to simmer, releasing its enchanting aromas, for 10 minutes.

Pour in the beef broth and bring the concoction to a gentle boil. Stir in the egg noodles, ensuring they're well submerged in the bubbling cauldron. Cover the skillet, reduce the heat to low, and let it all simmer until the noodles are tender—roughly 15 minutes.

Once the goulash is thick and hearty, stir in the sour cream for a creamy finish that will soothe even the most restless of spirits. Taste and adjust the seasoning if necessary.

Now, for the tombstones: Preheat your oven to 350°F. Brush the bread slices with melted butter and place them on a baking sheet. Bake until golden and crisp, about 10 minutes. Arrange them atop your goulash, standing upright for a spooky graveyard effect.

Savor this hauntingly delicious dish, where every bite is an adventure into the whimsical world of Halloween. May your goulash bewitch your senses and bring a smile to the faces of all who dare to try it. Until next time, happy haunting!

36. Bewitched Burgers

On a moonlit Halloween night, as the winds whisper secrets of ancient spells, what could be more enchanting than crafting a platter of Bewitched Burgers? These deliciously spooky delights are sure to cast a spell on both young and old, making your gathering truly magical.

Preparation time: 20 minutes
Cooking time: 15 minutes
Ready-in time: 35 minutes
Serving size: 4 people

Ingredients:
1 pound ground beef
1 teaspoon garlic powder
1 teaspoon onion powder
1/2 teaspoon smoked paprika
Salt and freshly ground black pepper, to taste
4 slices of cheddar cheese
4 hamburger buns
Lettuce leaves
4 slices of tomato
1/2 cup mayonnaise
2 tablespoons ketchup
1 tablespoon mustard
8 black olives, pitted
1 small cucumber, sliced into rounds
4 wooden skewers

Instructions:

Let's begin by setting the scene for a thrilling culinary adventure! In a large mixing bowl, combine the ground beef with garlic powder, onion powder, smoked paprika, salt, and pepper. Mix gently but thoroughly, ensuring the spices are evenly distributed. Now, form the mixture into four equal patties, each about half an inch thick.

Heat a skillet over medium-high heat. Once hot, place the patties in the skillet, cooking them for about 4 minutes on each side or until they reach your desired level of doneness. Just before they're ready, place a slice of cheddar cheese on each patty, allowing it to melt into a gooey, irresistible layer.

While the patties cook, let's prepare the buns. Toast them lightly, giving them a golden hue. Now, the magical touch: mix mayonnaise, ketchup, and mustard in a small bowl. Spread this enchanting sauce on the bottom half of each bun.

To assemble, lay a crisp lettuce leaf and a juicy tomato slice onto the sauce-coated buns. Gently place the cheesy patty on top. For the pièce de résistance, use black olives and cucumber slices on skewers to craft spooky eyes, piercing them through the top bun. Secure this top bun onto your patty creation.

And there you have it—a Bewitched Burger that is as delightful to the eyes as it is to the taste buds!

"Gather your little goblins and ghouls, and let the feast begin! These Bewitched Burgers are sure to disappear as quickly as a witch on a broomstick. Enjoy the magical mealtime moments that bring laughter and joy to your haunted festivities!

37. Ghastly Grilled Chicken

As the moon begins its mysterious ascent, conjure a Halloween feast that is both spine-tingling and delectable. This Ghastly Grilled Chicken promises to enchant your taste buds with its smoky allure and hauntingly delightful flavors.

Preparation time: 15 minutes
Cooking time: 30 minutes
Ready-in time: 45 minutes
Serving size: 4 people

Ingredients:
4 boneless, skinless chicken breasts
1/4 cup olive oil
3 tablespoons balsamic vinegar
1 tablespoon Worcestershire sauce
2 garlic cloves, minced
1 teaspoon smoked paprika
1 teaspoon dried thyme
Salt and freshly ground black pepper, to taste
1 lemon, sliced
Fresh parsley, for garnish

Instructions:

Now, gather your ingredients and let the magic begin. In a medium bowl, whisk together the olive oil, balsamic vinegar, Worcestershire sauce, minced garlic, smoked paprika, and dried thyme. This aromatic potion will be the key to your chicken's enchanting flavor.

Place the chicken breasts in a shallow dish and pour the marinade over them, ensuring each piece is thoroughly coated. Sprinkle with a pinch of salt and a dash of freshly ground black pepper. Cover and allow the chicken to marinate in the refrigerator for at least 15 minutes, though if you have the patience, an hour will deepen the spell.

As the evening draws near, preheat your grill to medium-high heat. While the grill heats, remove the chicken from the marinade, letting any excess drip off. Place the chicken on the grill, and let the sizzle commence. Grill each side for about 6 to 8 minutes, until the chicken is cooked through and boasts those charred, ghostly grill marks.

Once done, transfer the chicken to a platter. Squeeze the lemon slices over the top for a zesty twist and garnish with freshly chopped parsley. The result is a dish that's as delicious as it is hair-raising.

Serve this ghastly creation with your favorite sides, and watch as your family and friends delight in every spooky bite. Remember, a touch of fright makes the meal just right. Happy haunting, and may your Halloween be as flavorful as it is fun!

38. Trick-or-Treat Tacos

As the autumn leaves crackle underfoot and the air is laced with a hint of mischief, why not bring a touch of whimsy to your dinner table with these delightful Trick-or-Treat Tacos? They promise to be as enchanting as a moonlit night and as enjoyable as a good ghost story.

Preparation time: 20 minutes
Cooking time: 15 minutes
Ready-in time: 35 minutes
Serving size: 4 people

Ingredients:
1 tablespoon olive oil
1 pound ground beef
1 small onion, finely chopped
2 cloves garlic, minced
1 tablespoon taco seasoning
1 cup canned black beans, rinsed and drained
8 small corn tortillas
1 cup shredded cheddar cheese
1 cup sour cream
1 cup guacamole
1 cup salsa
1 cup shredded lettuce
1/2 cup cherry tomatoes, halved
1/4 cup black olives, sliced

Instructions:

First, let's take a moment to appreciate the simplicity of this delightful dish. Begin by heating the olive oil in a skillet over medium heat. Once it shimmers, add the ground beef, breaking it apart with a wooden spoon. As the beef browns, add the finely chopped onion and minced garlic, allowing them to become fragrant and translucent—a lovely aroma to fill your kitchen.

Now, sprinkle in the taco seasoning, stirring to ensure every morsel of beef is coated in its savory splendor. Introduce the black beans to the party, letting them warm through. This ensemble creates a filling that's both hearty and flavorful.

While the beef mixture simmers to perfection, let's turn our attention to the tortillas. Heat them gently in a dry skillet or microwave until they are warm and pliable, ready to cradle the flavorful filling.

To assemble these charming tacos, place a scoop of the beef mixture into each tortilla. Top generously with shredded cheddar cheese, a dollop of sour cream, a spoonful of guacamole, and a splash of salsa. Add a sprinkle of shredded lettuce, a few cherry tomato halves, and a scattering of black olive slices for a delightful garnish.

Serve these Trick-or-Treat Tacos with a flourish, inviting your family to dive into their playful presentation and delicious taste.

Ah, the joys of a festive feast, where each bite is a celebration of flavors and fun. These tacos are sure to bring a smile to your face and perhaps a little spooky delight to your evening. Until next time, may your culinary adventures be as spirited as these tacos!

39. Sinister Sausage Bake

In the spirit of Halloween, our kitchen turns into a whimsical world where the ordinary becomes extraordinary. Today, we embark on a delightful adventure concocting a frightfully fun dish that brings a touch of eerie enchantment to your table—perfect for little goblins and ghouls alike!

Preparation time: 15 minutes
Cooking time: 40 minutes
Ready-in time: 55 minutes
Serving size: 4 people

Ingredients:
1 pound of spicy sausage links
1 large red onion, sliced into moons
1 red bell pepper, sliced into strips
1 yellow bell pepper, sliced into strips
2 cloves of garlic, minced
1 tablespoon olive oil
1 teaspoon smoked paprika
1 teaspoon dried oregano
Salt and freshly ground pepper, to taste
1 cup shredded mozzarella cheese
Fresh parsley, chopped, for garnish

Instructions:

Begin by preheating your oven to a cozy 375°F (190°C), setting the stage for this sinister symphony of flavors. In your favorite skillet, warm the olive oil over medium heat, inviting the sliced onion and peppers to join the party. Let them dance and sizzle until they are soft and slightly caramelized—about 5 minutes should do the trick.

Next, introduce the garlic, allowing it to mingle for a minute before adding the spicy sausage links. Cook the sausages until golden brown, flipping occasionally to ensure an even tan, for about 8 minutes. Sprinkle the smoked paprika and oregano over the mixture, seasoning generously with salt and pepper.

Transfer this aromatic ensemble into a baking dish, spreading it evenly. Shower the top with a generous amount of mozzarella cheese, ensuring it blankets the sausages and veggies lovingly. Slide the dish into your preheated oven, letting it bake for roughly 25 minutes, until the cheese is bubbling and golden, casting an irresistible spell over your kitchen.

Once baked to perfection, remove the dish from the oven and let it rest for a moment. Garnish with fresh parsley, adding a touch of green that contrasts beautifully with the cheese.

Gather your little monsters and watch their eyes widen with delight as they dig into this Sinister Sausage Bake. It's a dish that promises to bewitch their taste buds and leave a lingering sense of enchantment long after the last bite. Enjoy!

40. Phantom Pizza Pockets

When the moon casts its eerie glow and little ghosts and goblins emerge from the shadows, these Phantom Pizza Pockets are sure to enchant your taste buds. A delightful blend of spooky and scrumptious, this recipe will transform your kitchen into a cauldron of culinary creativity.

Preparation time: 20 minutes
Cooking time: 15 minutes
Ready-in time: 35 minutes
Serving size: 4 people

Ingredients:
1 package of refrigerated pizza dough
1 cup marinara sauce
1 cup shredded mozzarella cheese
1/2 cup sliced pepperoni
1/4 cup chopped black olives
1 egg, beaten
1 tablespoon olive oil
1 teaspoon dried oregano
A pinch of salt
A pinch of black pepper
Flour, for dusting

Instructions:

First, gather your ingredients and let's conjure up some culinary magic! Preheat your oven to a bewitching 400 degrees Fahrenheit. Lightly dust your countertop with flour, then roll out the pizza dough into a rectangle, about 1/4 inch thick.

Now, with a gentle hand, spread the marinara sauce over the dough, leaving a small border around the edges. Sprinkle the mozzarella cheese generously over the sauce, followed by the pepperoni slices and chopped black olives. Sprinkle with a pinch of salt, black pepper, and dried oregano for a touch of aromatic wonder.

Carefully, fold the dough over the filling to create a pocket, pinching the edges securely. Use a fork to seal the edges, ensuring no delightful filling escapes. Brush the top of each pocket with the beaten egg to give it a glossy, golden finish.

Place your Phantom Pizza Pockets on a parchment-lined baking sheet, then drizzle with a whisper of olive oil. Slide them into the oven and bake for 15 minutes, or until the pockets are puffed and golden brown.

Let them cool for a few moments before serving. The aroma alone is enough to summon eager little monsters to the table!

Ah, you've done it! A hauntingly delicious treat that will have everyone under your spell. Enjoy the spooky delights and watch as your guests devour these Phantom Pizza Pockets with ghoulish glee. Remember, a little creativity can turn any meal into a festive celebration.

41. Witch's Finger Cookies

As the moonlight casts its eerie glow upon your kitchen, gather 'round to conjure up a batch of Witch's Finger Cookies. These ghoulish treats are sure to send delightful shivers down the spines of both the young and the young at heart.

Preparation time: 20 minutes
Cooking time: 20 minutes
Ready-in time: 1 hour
Serving size: 4 people

Ingredients:
1 cup unsalted butter, softened
1 cup powdered sugar
1 large egg
1 teaspoon vanilla extract
1 teaspoon almond extract
2 2/3 cups all-purpose flour
1 teaspoon baking powder
1 teaspoon salt
Green food coloring
Whole almonds
Red decorating gel

Instructions:

First, in a large mixing bowl, cream together the softened butter and powdered sugar until the mixture is light and fluffy. Now, add the egg, vanilla extract, and almond extract, blending everything until it's perfectly smooth. In a separate bowl, whisk together the flour, baking powder, and salt. Gradually add this dry mixture to the wet ingredients, mixing until the dough forms.

Add a few drops of green food coloring to the dough, mixing until you achieve a ghastly green hue. Once your dough is ready, cover it with plastic wrap and let it rest in the refrigerator for about 30 minutes.

Preheat your oven to 325°F (165°C) and line a baking sheet with parchment paper. Now, it's time to roll the dough! Take a small piece of dough and shape it into a finger-like cylinder, about 3 inches long. Press a whole almond at one end for the fingernail. Use a toothpick or knife to make shallow lines on the finger to create knuckles.

Place your eerie fingers on the prepared baking sheet, allowing room for them to expand. Bake for 20 minutes or until they are lightly golden. Once baked, let them cool on a wire rack. Finally, for that extra touch of spookiness, use red decorating gel around the base of the almond to resemble blood.

With your Witch's Finger Cookies complete, you've not only created a delicious treat but also added a spine-chilling centerpiece to your Halloween festivities. May your home be filled with laughter, joy, and just the right amount of fright this spooky season!

42. Creepy Crawly Cupcakes

In the spirit of Halloween, let's dive into a whimsical world where cupcakes meet creatures of the night. These Creepy Crawly Cupcakes are sure to enchant and perhaps even spook your family and friends with their delightful yet eerie appearance.

Preparation time: 20 minutes
Cooking time: 25 minutes
Ready-in time: 45 minutes
Serving size: 4 people

Ingredients:
1 cup all-purpose flour
1/2 cup unsweetened cocoa powder
1 teaspoon baking powder
1/2 teaspoon baking soda
1/4 teaspoon salt
1/2 cup unsalted butter, softened
3/4 cup granulated sugar
2 large eggs
1 teaspoon vanilla extract
1/2 cup buttermilk
1 cup chocolate frosting
Black decorating gel
Assorted gummy worms and candy spiders
Green sprinkles

Instructions:

First, let's get our oven preheated to a cozy 350 degrees Fahrenheit. In a bowl, whisk together the flour, cocoa powder, baking powder, baking soda, and salt until well combined. In another larger bowl, cream the butter and sugar together until light and fluffy. Then, add the eggs one at a time, ensuring each is well incorporated before moving on. Stir in the vanilla extract. Now, gently alternate adding the dry ingredients and buttermilk to your wet mixture, beginning and ending with the dry ingredients.

Spoon the batter into a cupcake tin lined with paper liners, filling each about two-thirds full. Bake for about 20 to 25 minutes, or until a toothpick inserted into the center of a cupcake comes out clean. Let them cool on a wire rack before the real fun begins.

Once cooled, frost each cupcake with a generous swirl of chocolate frosting. Now, the creative part: use the black decorating gel to create a spooky backdrop atop the frosting. Position your gummy worms to appear as if they're wriggling out of the cupcakes, and perch the candy spiders to add an extra touch of creepiness. Finish with a playful sprinkle of green sprinkles to mimic grass or moss.

These cupcakes are not just a treat for the taste buds, but a feast for the eyes. As you sink your teeth into these delightful creations, enjoy the playful fright they bring, and let your imagination run wild. Happy haunting!

43. Ghostly Gooey Brownies

As the moonlight casts its eerie glow, gather around the kitchen counter for a baking adventure that promises both thrills and chills. These spectral, gooey brownies will enchant little ghouls and goblins, making Halloween night a spooktacular memory for your family.

Preparation time: 15 minutes
Cooking time: 25 minutes
Ready-in time: 40 minutes
Serving size: 4 people

Ingredients:
1/2 cup unsalted butter, melted
1 cup granulated sugar
2 large eggs
1 teaspoon vanilla extract
1/3 cup unsweetened cocoa powder
1/2 cup all-purpose flour
1/4 teaspoon salt
1/4 teaspoon baking powder
1/2 cup semi-sweet chocolate chips
1/2 cup mini marshmallows

Instructions:

First, let's preheat that oven to a cozy 350 degrees Fahrenheit. As it warms, take a moment to prepare a square baking pan by lining it with parchment paper—this will make for an easy, ghostly escape once our brownies are baked.

In a medium mixing bowl, whisk together the melted butter and granulated sugar until they unite in a smooth, glossy concoction. Add the eggs one by one, stirring gently after each addition. Now, introduce a dash of vanilla extract to the mix, letting its sweet aroma fill the air.

Next, sift in the cocoa powder, flour, salt, and baking powder. Stir with care until the ingredients meld into a rich, chocolatey batter. At this point, fold in the semi-sweet chocolate chips, ensuring they're evenly distributed throughout the mixture.

Pour the batter into the prepared pan, smoothing the surface with a spatula. Sprinkle the mini marshmallows across the top, as if scattering cottony clouds over a dark night sky.

Slide the pan into the oven and bake for 25 minutes, or until the marshmallows puff and turn golden, creating a ghostly, gooey layer atop your brownies. Allow them to cool slightly in the pan before lifting them out using the parchment paper.

Now, it's time to slice and serve these hauntingly delicious treats. As you and your family indulge in these ghostly delights, remember: sometimes the spookiest nights lead to the sweetest memories. Happy haunting, dear bakers!

44. Monster Munch Popcorn

In the spirit of Halloween, let's transform humble popcorn into a delightful cauldron of sweet and salty enchantments. This Monster Munch Popcorn is sure to be the life of your spooky gathering, casting a spell on both young ghouls and seasoned specters alike with its whimsical charm.

Preparation time: 10 minutes
Cooking time: 15 minutes
Ready-in time: 25 minutes
Serving size: 4 people

Ingredients:
6 cups popped popcorn
1 cup pretzel twists
1 cup candy corn
1 cup mini marshmallows
1 cup chocolate chips
1/4 cup unsalted butter
1/4 cup light corn syrup
1/4 cup granulated sugar
1 teaspoon vanilla extract
1/2 teaspoon salt

Instructions:

Begin by preheating your oven to 300°F (150°C), setting the scene for a delightful treat. Place your popped popcorn and pretzel twists in a large, inviting mixing bowl. In a medium saucepan, melt the butter on low heat, allowing it to become a silky pool. Stir in the corn syrup and sugar, and raise the heat just a touch, coaxing the mixture to a gentle boil. Let it bubble for about two minutes, creating a fragrant, golden syrup.

Remove the saucepan from the heat and stir in the vanilla extract and salt, infusing the mixture with a cozy warmth. Pour this luscious concoction over the popcorn and pretzels, draping them in a glossy embrace. With a gentle hand, toss everything together until each kernel and twist is thoroughly coated in sweet delight.

Spread the mixture onto a baking sheet lined with parchment paper, ensuring an even layer. Bake in your preheated oven for about 10 minutes, stirring halfway through to ensure a perfect crunch. Once done, swiftly remove from the oven and let it cool slightly.

Now, let's add the finishing touches. Sprinkle the candy corn, mini marshmallows, and chocolate chips over the warm popcorn mixture, creating a kaleidoscope of Halloween colors. Let it cool completely on the baking sheet before transferring to a festive serving bowl.

"Gather your little monsters and enjoy this bewitching treat. Each bite is a delightful surprise, offering a medley of textures and flavors. Happy haunting, and may your Halloween be filled with sweet memories!

45. Spooky Spiderweb Cake

In the spirit of enchantment and a sprinkle of mystery, we embark on a culinary adventure, crafting a cake that embodies the whimsical allure of Halloween. Join me as we weave a web of deliciousness, perfect for captivating young ghouls and goblins alike.

Preparation time: 30 minutes
Cooking time: 45 minutes
Ready-in time: 1 hour 30 minutes
Serving size: 4 people

Ingredients:
1 1/2 cups all-purpose flour
1 cup granulated sugar
1/2 cup unsweetened cocoa powder
1 teaspoon baking powder
1/2 teaspoon baking soda
1/4 teaspoon salt
2 large eggs
1/2 cup buttermilk
1/2 cup vegetable oil
1 teaspoon vanilla extract
3/4 cup boiling water
1/2 cup semi-sweet chocolate chips
1/2 cup heavy cream
1/2 cup white chocolate chips
Black food coloring gel

Instructions:

Let's begin, shall we? First, preheat your oven to 350°F (175°C) and grease an 8-inch round cake pan with butter, then line it with parchment paper. In a large bowl, whisk together the flour, sugar, cocoa powder, baking powder, baking soda, and salt.

In another bowl, combine the eggs, buttermilk, vegetable oil, and vanilla extract, mixing until smooth. Gently fold the wet ingredients into the dry ones, ensuring a harmonious blend. Now, here's the secret: gradually stir in the boiling water to achieve a luscious, smooth batter. Pour this delightful concoction into your prepared pan.

Bake for 45 minutes, until a toothpick inserted in the center emerges clean. Allow the cake to cool in the pan for a spell, then transfer it to a wire rack.

For the ganache, heat the heavy cream in a small saucepan over medium heat until it simmers. Pour it over the semi-sweet chocolate chips in a bowl, stirring until glossy and smooth. Let it cool slightly before spreading over the cooled cake.

For our spiderweb magic, melt the white chocolate chips and mix with a drop of black food coloring gel. Transfer this potion to a piping bag with a small tip. On the ganache-coated cake, draw concentric circles, then drag a toothpick from the center outward to create a web effect.

Ah, the Spooky Spiderweb Cake is now ready to delight and surprise. As you indulge, remember that a touch of creativity and a dash of imagination can turn any treat into a festive masterpiece. Until our next culinary escapade, may your days be filled with sweet surprises!

46. Jack-O'-Lantern Orange Jelly

When Halloween whispers its approach, why not turn the ordinary into the extraordinary? Transform simple oranges into delightful Jack-O'-Lanterns filled with shimmering orange jelly. This whimsical treat will enchant little goblins and ghouls, making your Halloween gathering a magical memory.

Preparation time: 20 minutes
Cooking time: 10 minutes
Ready-in time: 3 hours
Serving size: 4 people

Ingredients:
4 large oranges
1 cup orange juice
1/2 cup granulated sugar
2 tablespoons lemon juice
1 packet unflavored gelatin
1 cup water
Green food coloring (optional)

Instructions:

First, gather the oranges, as vibrant and fresh as the autumn harvest. Carefully slice off the tops, setting them aside like jaunty little hats. With a gentle hand, scoop out the succulent flesh, leaving behind a hollow shell—these will become our charming Jack-O'-Lanterns.

Now, in a saucepan, combine the orange juice, sugar, and lemon juice. Over medium heat, stir until the sugar dissolves, creating a fragrant concoction that sings of citrus. Meanwhile, in a separate bowl, sprinkle the gelatin over water, allowing it to bloom for a few minutes.

Once the gelatin has softened, introduce it to the warm orange mixture. Stir lovingly until the gelatin dissolves completely, leaving no trace behind. For a playful touch, add a drop or two of green food coloring, if desired.

Pour this liquid sunshine into your hollowed orange shells, filling them almost to the brim. Gently place the tops back on, as if tucking them in for a cozy nap. Allow these jellied wonders to set in the fridge for a few hours, until they're firm and ready to delight.

Finally, before serving, carve delightful faces into the oranges, revealing the gleaming jelly within. Your Jack-O'-Lantern Oranges are now ready to charm and delight!

"Ah, the sweet success of transforming the humble orange into a Halloween spectacle! Enjoy these delightful treats, and relish the smiles and giggles they inspire. Happy haunting!

47. Eyeball Trifle

On a crisp autumn evening, invite a sense of whimsy and wonder into your kitchen with this delightfully eerie Eyeball Trifle. As the witching hour approaches, gather your little ghosts and goblins for a spine-tingling treat that is as fun to make as it is to eat!

Preparation time: 20 minutes
Cooking time: 10 minutes
Ready-in time: 30 minutes
Serving size: 4 people

Ingredients:
1 cup heavy whipping cream
2 tablespoons powdered sugar
1 teaspoon vanilla extract
1 package (3.4 oz) instant vanilla pudding mix
2 cups cold milk
1 cup strawberry or raspberry jam
8 large marshmallows
8 chocolate chips
1 cup crushed chocolate cookies
8 small clear plastic cups

Instructions:

First, begin by whipping up a delightful cloud of sweetness. In a chilled mixing bowl, combine the heavy whipping cream, powdered sugar, and vanilla extract. Whip these together until soft peaks form, then set this airy concoction aside for a moment.

Next, let's turn our attention to creating a luscious pudding layer. In a separate bowl, whisk the instant vanilla pudding mix with cold milk, stirring until it thickens beautifully. This will serve as the creamy foundation for our spooky trifle.

Now, for a bit of creepy charm, spoon a tablespoon of strawberry or raspberry jam into each clear plastic cup, allowing it to ooze down the sides for a gory effect. Over this, layer a generous scoop of the vanilla pudding, smoothing it with the back of a spoon.

To create the eyeballs, take each marshmallow and press a chocolate chip into its center, chocolate side down, forming a pupil. Nestle these into the pudding layer, pressing gently so they peek out eerily.

For a touch of dirt, sprinkle the crushed chocolate cookies over the pudding and eyeballs, adding texture and a delightful crunch. Finally, crown your creation with a dollop of the whipped cream you prepared earlier, swirling it to perfection.

Serve these creepy concoctions immediately, or refrigerate them until the little monsters are ready to enjoy.

Gather 'round and relish the delight of these spooky spectacles, a treat that promises giggles and gasps in equal measure. As the evening draws near, may your kitchen be filled with the magic of Halloween and the joy of shared moments. Until next time, happy haunting!

eyeballs

48. Black Cat Cookies

Halloween is a time when magic is in the air, and these Black Cat Cookies will add a delightful touch to your spooky gatherings. Crafted with whimsy and a sprinkle of enchantment, they are sure to make little eyes light up with delight.

Preparation time: 20 minutes
Cooking time: 12 minutes
Ready-in time: 32 minutes
Serving size: 4 people

Ingredients:
1 cup unsalted butter, softened
1 cup granulated sugar
1 large egg
2 teaspoons vanilla extract
2 1/2 cups all-purpose flour
1/2 cup unsweetened cocoa powder
1/2 teaspoon baking soda
1/4 teaspoon salt
Black food coloring gel
1/4 cup mini chocolate chips
1/4 cup candy eyes

Instructions:

Now, let's begin by preheating your oven to 350°F (175°C). As you do this, picture the magical transformation of simple ingredients into charming little black cats. In a large mixing bowl, with the help of an electric mixer, cream together the softened butter and sugar until light and fluffy. This is where the magic starts. Add in the egg and vanilla extract, mixing well until fully incorporated.

In a separate bowl, whisk together the flour, cocoa powder, baking soda, and salt. Gradually add this dry mixture to the creamed butter mixture, blending until a dough forms. To give our cookies their midnight hue, knead in the black food coloring gel until the dough reaches your desired shade.

Now, shape the dough into 1-inch balls and place them onto a baking sheet lined with parchment paper. Gently flatten each ball to form a circle. For the ears, pinch the top part of each circle to create two pointed ears. Press mini chocolate chips into the dough for the nose, and add candy eyes to bring your black cats to life.

Bake in the preheated oven for about 12 minutes, until the cookies are set. Once baked, allow them to cool on the baking sheet for a few minutes before transferring them to a wire rack to cool completely.

And there you have it, bewitching Black Cat Cookies that will surely be a delightful treat for your Halloween festivities.

With these charming cookies, you've conjured a little bit of magic right in your kitchen. Enjoy the sweet enchantment of Halloween, and may your celebration be as delightful and spirited as these Black Cat Cookies!

49. Mummy Marshmallow Pops

As the golden leaves crunch underfoot and the cool breeze whispers of tales untold, what better way to celebrate the spookiest time of year than with a treat that tickles the imagination and delights the taste buds? Enter the Mummy Marshmallow Pop—a delightful fusion of fright and fun.

Preparation time: 20 minutes
Cooking time: 0 minutes
Ready-in time: 20 minutes
Serving size: 4 people

Ingredients:
8 large marshmallows
8 lollipop sticks
1 cup white chocolate chips
2 teaspoons coconut oil
16 candy eyes
1 small tube of black decorating gel
1 cup graham cracker crumbs (optional)

Instructions:

Begin by gently inserting a lollipop stick into each marshmallow, taking care not to pierce all the way through. This is our base, the soft and fluffy heart of our mummy creation. Now, in a small microwave-safe bowl, combine the white chocolate chips and coconut oil. Microwave in 20-second intervals, stirring between each, until the mixture is smooth and gloriously glossy.

Once your chocolate is ready, it's time to coat the marshmallows. Dip each marshmallow into the melted chocolate, allowing the excess to drip back into the bowl. For those seeking a bit of crunch, roll the chocolate-coated marshmallows in graham cracker crumbs for a toasty touch.

Place the chocolate-dipped marshmallows on a parchment-lined tray, and while the chocolate is still melty, affix two candy eyes to each one. Now, for the pièce de résistance: using the black decorating gel, gently pipe lines across the chocolate, mimicking the ancient bandages of our mummified friends.

Allow your creations to set for about 10 minutes in the refrigerator, where they'll transform from mere marshmallows into delightful mummies ready to enchant any Halloween gathering.

With these delightful Mummy Marshmallow Pops, you're sure to conjure up smiles and perhaps a few playful shrieks. As the evening draws close, may your festivities be as enchanting as a moonlit ghost story. Happy haunting, dear friends!

50. Haunted Haystack Treats

In the spirit of all things spooky and delightful, let's weave together a fantastical treat that will enchant goblins and ghouls of all ages. Imagine crisp autumn leaves underfoot and a playful chill in the air as you whip up these spine-tingling haystack delights in your cozy kitchen.

Preparation time: 15 minutes
Cooking time: 5 minutes
Ready-in time: 20 minutes
Serving size: 4 people

Ingredients:
2 cups chow mein noodles
1 cup butterscotch chips
1 cup mini marshmallows
1/2 cup creamy peanut butter
1/4 cup candy corn
1/4 cup chocolate chips
Optional: a sprinkle of edible glitter for a magical touch

Instructions:
Begin by gathering your ingredients, letting the anticipation of spooky fun build. In a large, microwave-safe bowl, combine the butterscotch chips and creamy peanut butter. Now, pop the bowl into the microwave and melt them gently on medium power, stirring every 30 seconds until they blend into a smooth, golden mixture.

Once your concoction is ready, invite the mini marshmallows to join the party. Stir them in until they're well-coated, adding a touch of gooey delight to the mix. Now, introduce the chow mein noodles, folding them in ever so gently. Watch as they transform into a tangled web of sweet, crunchy goodness.

With your mixture ready, it's time to shape these eerie edibles. On a baking sheet lined with parchment paper, drop spoonfuls of the haystack mixture, forming small mounds that resemble mysterious haystacks under a moonlit sky. As a final flourish, press a few pieces of candy corn and chocolate chips into each haystack. If you're feeling particularly enchanting, sprinkle a touch of edible glitter over the top.

Allow these haunted haystacks to cool and set for about 15 minutes, though I promise the wait will be worth every spooky second.

With these Haunted Haystack Treats, you've spun a web of Halloween magic that's sure to delight all who dare to take a bite. Revel in the joy of creating memories that will linger long after the last treat disappears into the night!

51. Vampire Bite Red Velvet Cake

As the moon casts eerie shadows and little ghosts and goblins roam, what could be more delightfully chilling than a crimson-hued cake with a bite as sharp as a vampire's fang? This red velvet treat is a thrilling centerpiece for any spooky gathering.

Preparation time: 20 minutes
Cooking time: 30 minutes
Ready-in time: 1 hour
Serving size: 4 people

Ingredients:
1 and 1/4 cups all-purpose flour
1 tablespoon unsweetened cocoa powder
1/2 teaspoon baking soda
1/4 teaspoon salt
3/4 cup granulated sugar
1/2 cup unsalted butter, softened
1 large egg
1 teaspoon vanilla extract
1/2 cup buttermilk
2 teaspoons red food coloring
1 teaspoon white vinegar
1/4 cup cream cheese, softened
1/4 cup powdered sugar
1/4 teaspoon vanilla extract
1 tablespoon raspberry jam

Instructions:

Let's begin our delightful creation by preheating the oven to 350°F (175°C). Grease and flour a 9-inch round cake pan, ensuring every crevice is lovingly coated. In a medium bowl, whisk together the flour, cocoa powder, baking soda, and salt. This is your dry mixture and the very essence of your cake's structure.

In a large mixing bowl, beat the granulated sugar and butter until they become one, light and fluffy, like a cloud in the night sky. Add the egg and vanilla extract, mixing until just combined. It's time to introduce our red food coloring, a vibrant splash that will make our cake the talk of the evening.

Now, alternate adding the dry mixture and buttermilk to the batter, starting and ending with the flour mixture. Stir in the white vinegar with a gentle hand, as if casting a delicate spell. Pour this enchanting batter into your prepared cake pan, smoothing it out with a spatula.

Bake for 30 minutes, or until a toothpick inserted into the center emerges with just a few crumbs. Allow the cake to cool completely on a wire rack, as anticipation builds.

While the cake cools, let's turn our attention to the frosting. Beat together the cream cheese, powdered sugar, and vanilla extract until silky smooth. Carefully spread this creamy layer over your cooled cake.

Finally, for the vampire's bite, drizzle the raspberry jam over the top, crafting fang-like streaks that cascade down the sides.

Ah, our Vampire Bite Red Velvet Cake is complete, ready to enchant and delight. As guests take a bite, may they feel the thrill of Halloween and the warmth of your creativity. Until we meet again, may your kitchen be as magical as your imagination!

52. Skull Sugar Cookies

In the spirit of Halloween, there's nothing quite like transforming a simple sugar cookie into a bewitching treat. With a sprinkle of magic and a touch of creativity, these Skull Sugar Cookies will delight both the young and the young at heart as they haunt your taste buds with sweetness.

Preparation time: 20 minutes
Cooking time: 10 minutes
Ready-in time: 1 hour
Serving size: 4 people

Ingredients:
1 cup unsalted butter, softened
1 cup granulated sugar
1 large egg
1 teaspoon vanilla extract
2 ¾ cups all-purpose flour
½ teaspoon baking powder
¼ teaspoon salt
Black royal icing
Edible black pearls or candies for decoration

Instructions:

First, my dear bakers, we shall begin by preheating our ovens to a toasty 350 degrees Fahrenheit. Now, in a large mixing bowl, cream the softened butter and sugar until the mixture is as fluffy as a cloud on a sunny day. Add in the egg and vanilla extract, blending them well with your buttery concoction.

Next, let's whisk together the flour, baking powder, and salt in a separate bowl. Gradually add these dry ingredients into your creamy mixture, stirring until it forms a soft dough that's eager to be shaped.

Gently roll out the dough on a lightly floured surface to about a quarter-inch thickness. Use a skull-shaped cookie cutter to carve out your eerie treats, placing them onto a baking sheet lined with parchment paper. Be sure to leave a little space between each, as they need room to breathe.

After a swift 10 minutes in the oven, your cookies will emerge golden and fragrant. Allow them to cool completely before adorning them with your artistic flair. Use the black royal icing to outline and fill the skulls, then place edible black pearls for eyes, giving each cookie its own ghoulish personality.

Ah, the joy of watching these whimsical skulls come to life! Remember, a sprinkle of imagination is the secret ingredient to every frightfully fun Halloween treat. Until next time, may your kitchen be filled with laughter and a touch of spooky delight.

53. Bewitched Banana Bread

In the heart of autumn, when leaves dance like specters and shadows grow long, there's magic to be found in the humble banana. This delightful Bewitched Banana Bread calls forth flavors that enchant both young ghouls and seasoned goblins alike, casting a spell of delectable taste and cozy warmth.

Preparation time: 15 minutes
Cooking time: 1 hour
Ready-in time: 1 hour and 15 minutes
Serving size: 4 people

Ingredients:
3 ripe bananas, mashed
1/3 cup melted butter
1 teaspoon baking soda
Pinch of salt
3/4 cup sugar
1 large egg, beaten
1 teaspoon vanilla extract
1 1/2 cups all-purpose flour
1/2 cup chopped walnuts (optional, for extra crunch)
1/2 teaspoon cinnamon
1/4 teaspoon nutmeg
A handful of chocolate chips (for a touch of mystery)

Instructions:

Begin your culinary enchantment by preheating your oven to a toasty 350°F (175°C), letting its warmth fill your kitchen like a cauldron bubbling with potion. Prepare a 4x8-inch loaf pan, greasing it lovingly to ensure your magical creation doesn't stick.

In a mixing bowl, combine the mashed bananas with melted butter, stirring until they meld into a smooth potion. Sprinkle in the baking soda and a pinch of salt, and watch as the mixture begins to bubble with anticipation.

Next, whisk in the sugar, beaten egg, and vanilla extract, each adding their own charm to this beguiling batter. Gently fold in the flour, taking care not to disturb the spellbinding process. For an extra touch of enchantment, stir in the optional walnuts, cinnamon, nutmeg, and, of course, the chocolate chips.

Pour your bewitching batter into the prepared loaf pan, smoothing the top with a spatula as if casting a final spell. Slide it into the oven, where it will bake for about 60 minutes. You'll know it's done when a toothpick inserted into the center emerges clean, like a wizard's wand free of dark magic.

Once baked, allow your Bewitched Banana Bread to cool in the pan for a few minutes before transferring it to a wire rack. The aroma will be irresistible—like a siren's call to all who pass by.

Gather your little monsters and enjoy a slice of this magical bread. Watch as smiles spread like moonlight across their faces, and let the warmth of this delicious creation wrap around you like a cozy cloak. Until next time, may your culinary adventures always be spirited and delightful!

54. Creepy Chocolate Bark

Halloween beckons with its mysterious allure, and what better way to dive into the enchanting festivities than with a treat that combines whimsy and a touch of the macabre? This Creepy Chocolate Bark is sure to delight and spook your little goblins and ghosts alike.

Preparation time: 15 minutes
Cooking time: 5 minutes
Ready-in time: 1 hour
Serving size: 4 people

Ingredients:
8 ounces of dark chocolate, coarsely chopped
4 ounces of white chocolate, coarsely chopped
1/4 cup of candy eyeballs
1/4 cup of crushed pretzel sticks
1/4 cup of gummy worms
Sprinkles in Halloween colors (black, orange, purple)
A pinch of sea salt

Instructions:

First, let's prepare our canvas. Line a baking sheet with parchment paper and set it aside. This will be the stage for our eerie masterpiece.

Begin by melting the dark chocolate. Place it in a heatproof bowl set over a pot of simmering water. Stir gently until the chocolate is smooth and glossy. Alternatively, you can melt it in the microwave in 30-second intervals, stirring after each, until completely melted.

Now, pour the melted dark chocolate onto the prepared baking sheet. Use a spatula to spread it into a rectangle, approximately 1/4 inch thick. This will form the base of our bark.

Next, melt the white chocolate using the same method. Once melted, drizzle it over the dark chocolate base, creating a marbled effect. Use a toothpick to swirl the chocolates together, giving it a ghostly appearance.

While the chocolate is still warm, let's decorate! Scatter the candy eyeballs, crushed pretzel sticks, and gummy worms across the surface. Add a sprinkle of Halloween-colored sprinkles for a festive touch and finish with a pinch of sea salt to enhance the flavors.

Allow the chocolate bark to set at room temperature for about an hour, or place it in the refrigerator for faster setting. Once firm, break the bark into irregular pieces and serve.

Ah, the joy of crafting such delightful mischief! As your little ones bite into this spooky treat, watch their eyes widen with both fright and delight. Until our cauldrons bubble again, may your Halloween be as deliciously creepy as this chocolatey creation!

55. Graveyard Dirt Cups

In the spirit of Halloween, let's conjure a delightful treat that brings a playful fright to the dessert table. These Graveyard Dirt Cups are as fun to create as they are to devour, making them a spooktacular addition to any festive gathering.

Preparation time: 20 minutes
Cooking time: 0 minutes
Ready-in time: 20 minutes
Serving size: 4 people

Ingredients:
1 cup cold milk
1 package (3.9 ounces) chocolate instant pudding mix
2 cups whipped topping
16 chocolate sandwich cookies, crushed
1 cup gummy worms
4 graham crackers, broken into tombstone shapes
1 tube black gel icing

Instructions:

Begin by pouring the cold milk into a medium mixing bowl. Add the chocolate instant pudding mix and whisk together for about two minutes, or until it begins to thicken. As it sets, you'll see the magic start to happen, creating a deep, rich chocolate base for our eerie dessert. Once thickened, gently fold in the whipped topping; this will lend a light, creamy texture to our 'dirt'.

Now, it's time to prepare our graveyard. Take the chocolate sandwich cookies and place them in a resealable plastic bag. With a rolling pin, crush the cookies until they resemble fine dirt, then set them aside.

Layering is key in this creation: spoon a layer of the pudding mixture into four glasses or small mason jars, followed by a layer of crushed cookies. Repeat the process, ensuring the final layer is a generous sprinkle of 'dirt' on top.

To bring life to our graveyard, nestle a few gummy worms into the cookie layer, allowing them to peek out as if wriggling through the earth. Next, fashion tombstones from the graham crackers, using the black gel icing to inscribe spooky sayings or RIP on each. Gently press a tombstone into each cup, standing tall and proud as the centerpiece of your graveyard.

With a flourish, you've transformed simple ingredients into an enchanting Halloween spectacle. These Graveyard Dirt Cups invite young and old alike to indulge in their eerie allure, making them a perfect treat for a night of delightful fright. Enjoy the spooky sweetness, and may your Halloween be deliciously fun!

56. Eerie Eclairs

In the dim light of a crisp autumn evening, a touch of culinary magic can transform even the simplest treat into something delightfully spooky. This Halloween, let's conjure up some Eerie Eclairs that will enchant both young and old, bringing a playful dose of fright to your festive table.

Preparation time: 30 minutes
Cooking time: 25 minutes
Ready-in time: 1 hour
Serving size: 4 people

Ingredients:
1/2 cup water
1/4 cup unsalted butter
1/2 cup all-purpose flour
2 large eggs
1/2 teaspoon vanilla extract
1 cup heavy whipping cream
2 tablespoons powdered sugar
1/4 cup dark chocolate, melted
1/4 cup white chocolate, melted
Black and orange food coloring

Instructions:

Begin by preheating your oven to 400°F (200°C). In a sturdy saucepan over medium heat, combine the water and butter, waiting patiently as the butter melts and the mixture begins to simmer. Remove from the heat and swiftly stir in the flour until it forms a smooth ball. Now, let it cool for a few minutes.

Crack the eggs into a small bowl and whisk until combined. Gradually mix the eggs into the cooled dough, ensuring each addition is fully incorporated before adding the next. Stir in the vanilla extract for a hint of warmth. Transfer this choux pastry into a piping bag fitted with a large round tip.

On a baking sheet lined with parchment paper, pipe the dough into logs about 3 inches long. Bake for 20-25 minutes until the eclairs are golden and puffed. Allow them to cool on a wire rack.

While the eclairs cool, whip the heavy cream with the powdered sugar until soft peaks form. Divide the whipped cream into two bowls. Color one with black food coloring and the other with orange.

Slice the eclairs lengthwise and fill each with a swirl of the colored whipped cream. Drizzle the tops with melted dark chocolate, then playfully add some white chocolate drizzles, using a toothpick to create ghostly patterns.

Ah, behold your haunting creations! These Eerie Eclairs are sure to become the centerpiece of your Halloween festivities, enjoyed by all who dare to taste their spectral sweetness. May your celebrations be filled with laughter, delight, and just the right amount of fright!

57. Pumpkin Patch Pie

In the golden glow of autumn, when leaves crunch like crispy caramel wafers beneath our boots, we find the perfect time to indulge in a pie as playful as a pumpkin patch. This delightful creation will have you and your family skipping through the flavors of the season with every bite.

Preparation time: 20 minutes
Cooking time: 45 minutes
Ready-in time: 1 hour 15 minutes
Serving size: 4 people

Ingredients:
1 9-inch pie crust, store-bought or homemade
1 cup pumpkin puree
2/3 cup granulated sugar
1 teaspoon ground cinnamon
1/2 teaspoon ground ginger
1/4 teaspoon ground cloves
1/4 teaspoon salt
2 large eggs
3/4 cup evaporated milk
1 teaspoon vanilla extract
1/2 cup whipped cream, for serving
Handful of candy corn, for garnish

Instructions:

First, my dears, preheat your oven to a cozy 425 degrees Fahrenheit. Prepare your pie crust, gently laying it into your pie dish, and crimp the edges with the finesse of an artist sculpting their masterpiece. In a separate mixing bowl, whisk together the pumpkin puree, sugar, cinnamon, ginger, cloves, and salt, creating a velvety blend of autumnal aromas. Crack the eggs into the mixture, one at a time, whisking with a graceful rhythm until the concoction is smooth and inviting.

Now, gently fold in the evaporated milk and vanilla extract, turning the batter into a creamy elixir that promises pure delight. Pour this luscious filling into your prepared crust, smoothing the surface with the back of a spoon, as if you were painting a canvas with the colors of fall.

Slide your pie into the oven, and let it bake for 15 minutes. Then, reduce the temperature to 350 degrees Fahrenheit and continue baking for another 30 minutes, until the filling is set and a toothpick inserted in the center comes out clean. Allow the pie to cool on a wire rack, letting the flavors mingle and meld.

To serve, dollop each slice with a cloud of whipped cream, and sprinkle with candy corn, like tiny pumpkins scattered across a harvest field. As you slice into this Pumpkin Patch Pie, feel the joy of the pumpkin harvest imbue your spirit with warmth and cheer.

And there you have it, a sensational autumn treat that's as delightful to make as it is to eat! Now gather your little goblins and witches around the table and share in the magic of the season, one delicious slice at a time.

58. Sinister S'mores Bars

 # 58. Sinister S'mores Bars

As the autumn leaves rustle and shadows dance, there's nothing quite like the magical allure of a sweet treat with a devilish twist. These Sinister S'mores Bars are a delightful concoction, perfect for casting a spell on your taste buds during the Halloween season.

Preparation time: 20 minutes
Cooking time: 25 minutes
Ready-in time: 1 hour
Serving size: 4 people

Ingredients:
1 cup graham cracker crumbs
1/4 cup unsalted butter, melted
1/4 cup granulated sugar
1/2 cup semi-sweet chocolate chips
1/2 cup milk chocolate chips
1 cup mini marshmallows
1/2 cup caramel sauce
1/4 teaspoon sea salt
1/3 cup Halloween-themed sprinkles

Instructions:

Ah, the Sinister S'mores Bars—where chocolate, marshmallow, and caramel meet in a dance of delightful decadence. Share them with friends, family, or perhaps just enjoy them yourself as you sit by a flickering flame, savoring each bite. Until next time, happy haunting in the kitchen!

Let us begin with a delightful mixture of graham cracker crumbs, sugar, and melted butter. Blend these together until they resemble the texture of sand, then press this mixture firmly into an 8x8-inch baking dish to form the crust. This is your canvas, the foundation of our wickedly delicious creation.

Next, preheat your oven to 350°F (175°C). While that warms up, scatter the semi-sweet and milk chocolate chips over the crust, spreading them evenly—like stars in a dark, delicious sky.

Now, it's marshmallow time! Sprinkle the mini marshmallows generously over the chocolate layer. Do not be shy; the more marshmallows, the merrier the mischief.

Drizzle the gooey caramel sauce over the top, letting it weave between the marshmallows like a golden web. Finish with a sprinkle of sea salt, a hint of mystery to balance the sweetness.

Into the oven it goes! Bake for about 25 minutes, or until the marshmallows are toasted to a lovely golden brown, like a warm autumn sunset. Once done, remove from the oven and let it cool for at least 15 minutes. The hardest part is waiting, but patience is a virtue, they say.

Finally, sprinkle your Halloween-themed sprinkles over the top, adding a festive flair. Slice into bars and serve, watching as they disappear faster than a ghostly apparition.

59. Wicked Witch's Apple Crisp

As the autumn leaves rustle in the cool breeze and the shadows grow long, what better way to welcome the spooky season than with a dish that combines the enchantment of apples with a touch of magic? Let us conjure a dessert that is both wickedly delightful and irresistibly crisp.

Preparation time: 20 minutes
Cooking time: 40 minutes
Ready-in time: 1 hour
Serving size: 4 people

Ingredients:
4 medium apples, peeled, cored, and sliced thinly
1 tablespoon lemon juice
1/2 cup granulated sugar
1/2 teaspoon ground cinnamon
1/4 teaspoon nutmeg
1/3 cup all-purpose flour
1/3 cup old-fashioned rolled oats
1/4 cup packed brown sugar
1/4 teaspoon salt
1/4 cup unsalted butter, chilled and diced
1/4 cup chopped walnuts (optional)
Vanilla ice cream, for serving (optional)

Instructions:

Now, my dears, gather your ingredients and let us embark on this culinary adventure. Begin by preheating your oven to 350 degrees Fahrenheit. This will ensure our apple crisp bakes evenly to a golden perfection. As the oven warms, place your apple slices in a mixing bowl, tossing them with the lemon juice to preserve their vibrant hue. Sprinkle the granulated sugar, cinnamon, and nutmeg over the apples, giving them a gentle stir until each slice is cloaked in sweet spices.

In a separate bowl, whisk together the flour, oats, brown sugar, and salt. This will be our enchantingly crisp topping. Using your fingers or a pastry cutter, blend in the chilled butter until the mixture resembles coarse crumbs. If you fancy a bit of nutty crunch, add the walnuts at this stage.

Arrange the spiced apples in an even layer in a baking dish, then sprinkle the crumbly topping over them, letting it fall where it may. Place the dish into the preheated oven and allow it to bake for 40 minutes. You'll know it's ready when the apples are tender and the topping is a deep, caramelized brown.

Once your apple crisp has cooled slightly, serve it warm with a scoop of vanilla ice cream if you wish to indulge further.

And there you have it, a dessert so delightful it could charm even the most discerning witch. Enjoy this spellbinding treat with family and friends, and let it become a cherished tradition in your own haunt. Until next time, may your kitchen be filled with magic and mirth!

60. Phantom Pudding Parfaits

In the magical realm of Halloween, where shadows dance and whispers fill the night air, these Phantom Pudding Parfaits emerge as a delightful mystery. With layers as enchanting as a witch's spellbook, each spoonful reveals a sweet surprise, delighting ghouls and goblins of all ages.

Preparation time: 15 minutes
Cooking time: 10 minutes
Ready-in time: 25 minutes
Serving size: 4 people

Ingredients:
1 cup whole milk
1 cup heavy cream
1/2 cup granulated sugar
1 tablespoon vanilla extract
3 tablespoons cornstarch
A pinch of salt
A few drops of black food coloring
1 cup crushed chocolate cookies
1/2 cup whipped cream
Candy eyes or Halloween-themed sprinkles for decoration

Instructions:

Now, my dear friends, let us embark on our spooky culinary journey. Begin by whisking together the milk, heavy cream, granulated sugar, vanilla extract, cornstarch, and a pinch of salt in a medium saucepan. Place this delightful mixture over medium heat, stirring continuously. As the potion simmers, it will begin to thicken, forming a creamy, bewitching pudding.

Once thickened to perfection, remove the saucepan from the heat and divide the pudding into two bowls. In one bowl, add a few drops of black food coloring, stirring gently until you achieve a shadowy hue that would make even the most fearsome phantom proud.

Now, gather your parfait glasses—four, to be precise. Begin layering with a generous spoonful of the dark pudding at the bottom, followed by a layer of crushed chocolate cookies, the texture reminiscent of ancient, crumbling tombstones. Next, add a layer of the uncolored pudding, creating a haunting contrast.

Continue layering until your glasses are filled with this ghostly delight, ending with a dollop of whipped cream on top. For the final touch, adorn each parfait with candy eyes or Halloween-themed sprinkles, giving them an eerie gaze.

Refrigerate for a brief spell, about 10 minutes, allowing the flavors to meld and the parfaits to set. Now, gather your little ghosts and goblins, and indulge in this otherworldly treat.

Ah, wasn't that a charming and ghoulish adventure? These parfaits are sure to haunt your taste buds with their delightful layers. Until next time, may your kitchen be filled with magic and your heart with joy!

61. Witch's Brew Punch

When the moon is high and the shadows stretch long, there's nothing quite like a bubbling cauldron of Witch's Brew Punch to stir excitement at your Halloween gathering. With a hint of mystery and a splash of whimsy, this concoction promises to delight children of all ages.

Preparation time: 10 minutes
Cooking time: 0 minutes
Ready-in time: 10 minutes
Serving size: 4 people

Ingredients:
3 cups of cranberry juice
1 cup of orange juice
1 cup of lemon-lime soda
1/2 cup of pineapple juice
1/4 cup of grenadine syrup
1 cup of gummy worms
Ice cubes
Optional: a few drops of green food coloring

Instructions:

Begin by gathering your magical ingredients. In a large, enchanting bowl, pour the cranberry juice, orange juice, lemon-lime soda, and pineapple juice. Give it a gentle stir with a wooden spoon as if you were casting a spell. To add a splash of color and a dash of sweetness, drizzle in the grenadine syrup, watching as it swirls like a mystical potion.

Next, for a touch of eerie charm, sprinkle in a handful of gummy worms. They'll wriggle and writhe about, much to the delight of your young guests. If you're feeling particularly adventurous, add a few drops of green food coloring to enhance the brew's otherworldly hue.

Now, add a handful of ice cubes to keep your potion cool and refreshing. Stir gently, ensuring that all the flavors meld together seamlessly.

Once your brew is complete, ladle it into glasses, ensuring each serving boasts a few gummy worms for playful effect. Encourage little hands to reach for these sweet, squiggly surprises.

Remember, every sip should be savored, as if you were tasting a rare elixir crafted by a wise old witch.

Ah, the Witch's Brew Punch – a potion so enchanting, it's bound to bewitch your senses and leave everyone spellbound. As the laughter of little goblins and ghouls fills the air, this delightful punch will surely become a cherished part of your Halloween tradition.

62. Ghostly Green Smoothie

As the leaves turn crisp and the air fills with the whispers of autumn, why not conjure up a delightfully spooky treat to enchant your little ghouls? This Ghostly Green Smoothie is both a fright and a delight, casting a spell of health and flavor in every sip.

Preparation time: 10 minutes
Cooking time: 0 minutes
Ready-in time: 10 minutes
Serving size: 4 people

Ingredients:
1 cup fresh spinach leaves, washed
1 ripe banana, peeled
1 cup green grapes, seedless
1/2 cup Greek yogurt
1/2 cup coconut water
1 tablespoon honey
1/2 teaspoon vanilla extract
1/2 teaspoon spirulina powder (optional, for extra spookiness)
Ice cubes, as needed

Instructions:

First, gather all your ingredients and let the excitement of creating something ghostly take over. In the realm of your blender, place the fresh spinach leaves, allowing their vibrant green to take the lead in this spectral symphony. Next, break the banana into chunks, adding a sweet and creamy dimension to your potion.

Follow with the green grapes, their juicy burst perfectly complementing the otherworldly green. Now, invite the Greek yogurt for a creamy embrace and add the coconut water to ensure a smooth, flowing consistency. A drizzle of honey brings a touch of natural sweetness, while a hint of vanilla extract whispers of warmth and whimsy.

For those who dare, a dash of spirulina powder will deepen the hue, making your smoothie as mysterious as it is nourishing. Add a handful of ice cubes to chill your creation, making it refreshingly cool and perfectly suited for a Halloween haunt.

Secure the lid on your blender and, with a firm hand, blend everything together until you achieve a smooth, velvety consistency. Pour the ghostly green elixir into four glasses, ready to be enjoyed by eager hands.

And there you have it—a smoothie that's both ghoulishly green and delightfully delicious.

With this Ghostly Green Smoothie in hand, you'll be ready to face any Halloween haunt with a smile. Remember, the real magic lies in sharing these moments with those you love. Enjoy each sip, and let the spooky season unfold with joy and laughter!

63. Monster Milkshakes

Imagine a world where ghouls and goblins crave not for fright, but for delightful sips of monstrous concoctions. These Monster Milkshakes, a whimsical blend of gory garnishes and creamy delights, promise to enchant your taste buds and awaken the mischievous spirit of Halloween in every sip.

Preparation time: 10 minutes
Cooking time: 5 minutes
Ready-in time: 15 minutes
Serving size: 4 people

Ingredients:
2 cups vanilla ice cream
1 cup milk
1/2 cup heavy cream
1/4 cup chocolate syrup
Green food coloring
1/4 cup mini marshmallows
1/4 cup gummy worms
1/4 cup crushed chocolate cookies
Whipped cream, for topping
Candy eyes, for decoration

Instructions:

Now, let's embark on this magical journey of creating our Monster Milkshakes. Begin by placing the vanilla ice cream, milk, and heavy cream into a blender. Add a generous splash of chocolate syrup, then get a little playful with a few drops of green food coloring, just enough to achieve that eerie, ghoulish hue.

Secure the lid and blend until the mixture is smooth and frothy. Taste it—if it needs a bit more sweetness, feel free to add an extra drizzle of chocolate syrup. Next, prepare your serving glasses by swirling chocolate syrup around the inner sides, creating spooky patterns that will delight any little (or big) monster.

Pour the blended mixture carefully into each glass, filling them about three-quarters full. Now for the fun part—top each milkshake with a cloud of whipped cream, and go wild with your garnishes. Sprinkle mini marshmallows and crushed chocolate cookies over the top. Gently nestle gummy worms into the whipped cream, letting them dangle over the edges as if crawling from the depths. Finally, for that extra bit of whimsy, place candy eyes strategically on top of the whipped cream.

Serve these Monster Milkshakes with a straw and a spoon, and watch them disappear faster than a ghost at dawn.

With each sip, you'll find yourself enchanted by the playful blend of flavors and textures. Here's to creating memories as sweet as these milkshakes, and may your Halloween be filled with laughter and delightful frights!

64. Spooky Spider Lemonade

As the autumn leaves flutter and the moonlight dances upon the shadows, it's time to brew a potion of delight that's as enchanting as it is chilling. Embrace the playful eeriness of Halloween with a lemonade that's sure to weave a web of smiles and giggles.

Preparation time: 10 minutes
Cooking time: 5 minutes
Ready-in time: 15 minutes
Serving size: 4 people

Ingredients:
1 cup freshly squeezed lemon juice (about 4-5 lemons)
4 cups cold water
1 cup granulated sugar
1 teaspoon edible black glitter
Few drops of purple food coloring
Ice cubes
4 gummy spiders for garnish
Slices of lemon, for garnish

Instructions:

First, begin by creating a simple syrup. In a small saucepan over medium heat, combine the sugar with one cup of water. Stir gently until the sugar has dissolved completely—this should take around 5 minutes. Once achieved, set it aside to cool.

While your syrup cools, embrace the fresh citrus aroma and squeeze those lemons until you have a vibrant cup of juice. Combine this liquid sunshine with the remaining three cups of cold water in a pitcher. Now, introduce the cooled simple syrup to the mix, stirring until it's all beautifully blended.

For a touch of magic, sprinkle in the edible black glitter and add a few drops of purple food coloring. Stir gently, allowing the colors to swirl and dance like a witch's brew. Taste and adjust the sweetness to your liking—after all, each potion is unique to its creator.

To serve, fill each glass with ice cubes, pour over the spooky lemonade, and dare to garnish with gummy spiders and lemon slices. Watch as your little ghouls and goblins delight in their eerie refreshment.

Gather round, dear friends, and sip this spectral elixir as your tales of mischief and magic unfold. Remember, the most bewitching moments are crafted with a dash of creativity and a sprinkle of fun. Cheers to a Halloween filled with whimsy and wonder!

65. Vampire's Blood Mocktail

When the bewitching hour is upon us, and the little goblins are gathered around with expectant eyes, there's nothing quite like a Vampire's Blood Mocktail to set the scene. This eerie elixir is a delightful concoction, promising a little thrill with every sip.

Preparation time: 10 minutes
Cooking time: 0 minutes
Ready-in time: 10 minutes
Serving size: 4 people

Ingredients:
2 cups cranberry juice
1 cup pomegranate juice
1/2 cup sparkling water
1/4 cup freshly squeezed lime juice
1 tablespoon grenadine syrup
Crushed ice
Lime wedges, for garnish
Blackberries, for garnish

Instructions:

Let's begin by assembling our cauldron of flavors. In a large pitcher, combine the cranberry juice and pomegranate juice, stirring them together until they dance in harmony. Next, add the sparkling water, giving your concoction a delightful fizz that's sure to enchant. Pour in the freshly squeezed lime juice, which adds a refreshing zing, perfect for awakening the senses.

Now, the secret ingredient to give our mocktail its mysterious allure: grenadine syrup. Carefully drizzle it in, and watch as it swirls, creating a mesmerizing, blood-red hue that would make any vampire proud. Fill four glasses with crushed ice, and divide your mixture evenly among them, allowing an icy chill to enhance the experience.

Finally, it's time for a little embellishment. Garnish each glass with a lime wedge and a couple of plump blackberries, like tiny jewels crowning our drink. Now, stand back and admire your creation, perfect for any Halloween gathering.

With a wave of your hand and a touch of imagination, you've conjured up a mocktail that's both frightful and delightful. Cheers to a night filled with giggles and ghouls, and remember, a little spookiness makes everything more fun!

66. Haunted Hot Chocolate

On a crisp Halloween night, when the moon lights up the sky and the air is filled with mystery, nothing warms the soul quite like a cup of Haunted Hot Chocolate. It's a whimsical potion, sure to delight little goblins and ghouls with every spooky sip.

Preparation time: 10 minutes
Cooking time: 10 minutes
Ready-in time: 20 minutes
Serving size: 4 people

Ingredients:
4 cups whole milk
½ cup heavy cream
1 cup semi-sweet chocolate chips
1 tablespoon unsweetened cocoa powder
2 tablespoons sugar
1 teaspoon vanilla extract
A pinch of salt
Whipped cream for topping
Mini marshmallows
Chocolate syrup
Candy eyes

Instructions:

Begin by gathering your cauldron—well, a medium-sized saucepan will do for now—and pour in the whole milk and heavy cream. Set it over medium heat, stirring occasionally to keep the milk from scalding. As you watch the steam rise like eerie mists over a midnight marsh, add the semi-sweet chocolate chips, allowing them to melt slowly, infusing the milk with their rich, dark charm.

Once the chocolate has melted, sprinkle in the unsweetened cocoa powder and sugar, stirring with care to dissolve any lingering lumps. A pinch of salt will balance the sweetness, enhancing the deep, velvety notes of this bewitching brew. Now, add the vanilla extract for a touch of warmth, stirring gently as the flavors meld together.

As the potion simmers, prepare your goblets. Pour the steaming hot chocolate into each one, leaving just enough room at the top for a whimsical crown of whipped cream. Adorn each cup with a handful of mini marshmallows, letting them float like ghostly apparitions. Drizzle a delicate web of chocolate syrup over the top and, for a final touch, place a few candy eyes amid the marshmallows—the perfect finishing touch to this haunting delight.

With your Haunted Hot Chocolate in hand, gather around and share spine-tingling tales by candlelight. Let the warmth of the chocolate melt away the chills of the night, and remember—it's the little touches of magic that make Halloween a truly enchanting celebration.

67. Ghoul's Grape Fizz

In the spirit of Halloween, when the moon is high and shadows dance, let's concoct a bewitching brew that will delight young and old alike. Our Ghoul's Grape Fizz, with its whimsical bubbles and haunting hue, will surely enchant your family's festive gathering.

Preparation time: 10 minutes
Cooking time: 0 minutes
Ready-in time: 10 minutes
Serving size: 4 people

Ingredients:
2 cups grape juice
1 cup ginger ale
1 cup sparkling water
1 tablespoon lime juice
4 tablespoons blueberry syrup
Ice cubes
Gummy worms or eyeball candies for garnish

Instructions:

Begin by assembling your cauldron of concoctions, also known as a pitcher, and fill it with two cups of grape juice. This will serve as the midnight canvas for our mischievous potion. Next, introduce a cup of ginger ale, whose effervescent nature will lend our brew a delightful fizz.

Now, gently pour in a cup of sparkling water, enhancing the bubbling cauldron effect. A tablespoon of lime juice follows, adding a zesty zing that will elevate the flavors. Stir gently, allowing these elements to meld like a symphony of flavors.

To create a mysteriously vibrant hue, swirl in four tablespoons of blueberry syrup. Watch as it weaves through the liquid, creating an enchanting visual treat.

Once combined, fill each glass with ice cubes, constructing a chilly base for your Ghoul's Grape Fizz. Pour the mixture over the ice, letting it cascade into each glass with a satisfying fizz.

For the final touch, adorn each glass with gummy worms or eyeball candies, ensuring your creation looks as ghastly as it is delightful.

May your Halloween be filled with laughter and glee, as you sip on this concoction of mystery. Remember, the magic is in the moments we share, and with a Ghoul's Grape Fizz, those moments become unforgettable tales.

68. Jack-O'-Lantern Juice

A cool autumn breeze rustles the leaves as children carve their pumpkins with glee. Capture that whimsy in a glass with Jack-O'-Lantern Juice, a delightful concoction that bubbles with mystery and wonder. Gather your little goblins and witches for a bewitching treat that's sure to enchant.

Preparation time: 10 minutes
Cooking time: 0 minutes
Ready-in time: 10 minutes
Serving size: 4 people

Ingredients:
3 cups fresh orange juice
1 cup carrot juice
1/2 cup pineapple juice
1 tablespoon lemon juice
1/4 teaspoon ground ginger
1/4 teaspoon ground cinnamon
Orange slices, for garnish
Fresh mint leaves, for garnish

Instructions:

First, let's set the stage for this delicious potion. In a large pitcher, pour in the fresh orange juice. Ah, the scent of citrus is simply invigorating, isn't it? Now, add the carrot juice. Its vibrant color adds to the magic of our Jack-O'-Lantern Juice.

Next, stir in the pineapple juice. Imagine the tropical breeze joining our autumn adventure! Add the lemon juice, a splash of tangy brightness that wakes up the palate. Now, we want to sprinkle in the ground ginger and ground cinnamon. These spices bring warmth and a hint of mystery to our brew.

Using a long spoon, give the mixture a gentle stir. The colors and aromas mingle beautifully, creating a symphony of flavors. Pour the juice into chilled glasses, perhaps those with frosted rims for a touch of elegance.

To finish, adorn each glass with an orange slice and a sprig of fresh mint. The garnishes not only look festive but add a delightful aroma as you sip. Serve immediately to your eager guests, who will surely appreciate this enchanting elixir.

With every sip of Jack-O'-Lantern Juice, you and your guests will feel the magic of Halloween. Gather close and share your spookiest stories, knowing that the essence of autumn is captured perfectly in this bewitching beverage. Cheers to a delightful and deliciously eerie celebration!

69. Sinister Strawberry Slush

Amidst the eerie glow of jack-o'-lanterns, a foreboding chill sweeps through the air, whispering of a time when spooky treats reign supreme. What better way to celebrate than with a frosty concoction that looks as delightful as it is devilish? Unveil the magic of this ghoulishly good slush!

Preparation time: 15 minutes
Cooking time: 0 minutes
Ready-in time: 15 minutes
Serving size: 4 people

Ingredients:
2 cups fresh strawberries, hulled
1 cup cranberry juice
1 cup ice cubes
2 tablespoons honey or agave syrup
1 tablespoon fresh lemon juice
A few drops of red food coloring (optional)
Whipped cream, for garnish
Halloween-themed sprinkles, for garnish

Instructions:

Now, let's embark on this spooky culinary journey. First, gather your vibrant, ruby-red strawberries. Ensure they're hulled and ready to be transformed. Place them ever so gently into your blender, followed by a cup of refreshingly tart cranberry juice. Add the ice cubes, a crucial element in crafting that perfect slushy texture.

Next, introduce a touch of sweetness with two tablespoons of honey or agave syrup. This will dance harmoniously with the tartness of our berry concoction. A squeeze of fresh lemon juice will add a hint of zest, elevating the flavors to new, spine-tingling heights.

For those who wish to add an extra layer of sinister allure, a few drops of red food coloring can be blended in, but remember, a little goes a long way. Secure the lid of your blender, and pulse the mixture until it reaches a smooth, icy consistency.

Once your slush is ready, pour it carefully into chilled glasses, allowing the crimson hue to shine through. To finish, crown each glass with a dollop of whipped cream, and sprinkle with Halloween-themed sprinkles for a festive touch.

Serve immediately and let the chilling delight of the Sinister Strawberry Slush enchant your taste buds.

It's a treat that will surely have both goblins and ghouls coming back for more! Savor every sip, and watch as the magic of Halloween unfolds in each frosty, blood-red glass. Remember, the key to any good slush is a touch of mystery, a hint of sweetness, and a whole lot of fun!

70. Bewitched Berry Smoothie

In the realm of culinary magic, where flavors dance with the spirit of Halloween, lies a potion so enchanting it could charm even the most mischievous ghost. Gather your little wizards and witches, for this spellbinding beverage will transform your kitchen into a cauldron of berry bliss.

Preparation time: 10 minutes
Cooking time: 0 minutes
Ready-in time: 10 minutes
Serving size: 4 people

Ingredients:
2 cups frozen mixed berries
1 banana, peeled
1 cup vanilla yogurt
1 cup almond milk
2 tablespoons honey
1 teaspoon vanilla extract
A pinch of cinnamon
A handful of fresh mint leaves for garnish

Instructions:

Now, dear friends, it's time to conjure up our fruity elixir. Begin by summoning your trusted blender, that ever-so-helpful appliance of wonder. Into its depths, place the frozen mixed berries, allowing their icy allure to beckon. Add the banana, which brings a natural sweetness and creamy texture to our potion. Next, we incorporate the silky smoothness of vanilla yogurt, a delightful partner to our berry medley.

Pour in the almond milk, a gentle tide that will carry our flavors to new heights. Drizzle in the golden honey, a sweet touch that whispers of enchanted forests. Introduce a teaspoon of vanilla extract, offering warmth and depth to our creation. Finally, sprinkle a pinch of cinnamon, a spice as ancient and mysterious as the night itself.

Secure the lid on your blender and blend these ingredients until they meld into a velvety smoothie, a vibrant symphony of color and taste. Pour the potion into glasses, and for the final flourish, crown each with a sprig of fresh mint, a nod to the magic within.

May this berry concoction delight and surprise you, as it brings a touch of whimsy to your Halloween festivities. Savor each sip, and let it transport you to a world where every moment is a celebration of the season's enchantment. Until our next culinary adventure, enjoy the magic!

71. Phantom Fruit Punch

On a moonlit Halloween night, when the wind whispers secrets through the trees, a mysterious concoction awaits in the kitchen. Crafted with enchantment and a splash of mischief, this Phantom Fruit Punch is sure to mesmerize young and old alike with its tantalizing flavors and spooky charm.

Preparation time: 10 minutes
Cooking time: None
Ready-in time: 10 minutes
Serving size: 4 people

Ingredients:
2 cups cranberry juice
1 cup orange juice
1 cup pineapple juice
1 cup sparkling water
½ cup gummy worms
1 lime, thinly sliced
½ cup frozen blueberries
Ice cubes

Instructions:

Let us begin by gathering our vibrant elixirs and inviting them to dance together in a large punch bowl. Pour in the cranberry juice, orange juice, and pineapple juice, allowing their colors to swirl and mingle like a painter's palette. Next, gently introduce the sparkling water, creating a festive fizz that bubbles with delight.

Now, for a touch of whimsy, add the gummy worms—each one a playful surprise waiting to be discovered. Slice the lime into thin, delicate rounds and float them atop the liquid, their citrusy scent adding a fresh, aromatic note. Scatter the frozen blueberries across the surface, like tiny, dark orbs of mystery bobbing in an enchanting sea.

Finally, fill the bowl with ice cubes, giving our Phantom Fruit Punch a chill as refreshing as the autumn breeze. Stir with a wooden spoon, watching as the ingredients come together in a delightful, harmonious blend. Taste the punch and adjust its sweetness to your liking with a hint of honey or a sprinkle of sugar if needed.

As the punch is ready to serve, pour it into glasses and garnish with additional gummy worms for an extra dose of fun. Now, gather your friends and family, and let the festivities begin!

With each sip of this bewitching brew, may your Halloween be filled with laughter, mystery, and delightful moments shared with loved ones. Here's to a spooktacular celebration, where every sip brings a little magic to your night!

72. Creepy Cranberry Cider

As the leaves turn crisp and the moon casts its mysterious glow, there's nothing quite like a warm, spiced cider to evoke the spirit of Halloween. This Creepy Cranberry Cider not only warms your bones but also adds a spine-tingling twist to your festive celebrations.

Preparation time: 10 minutes
Cooking time: 30 minutes
Ready-in time: 40 minutes
Serving size: 4 people

Ingredients:
4 cups cranberry juice
2 cups apple cider
1/4 cup fresh orange juice
1/4 cup brown sugar
1 cinnamon stick
4 whole cloves
1 orange, thinly sliced
1/2 cup fresh or frozen cranberries
1/4 teaspoon ground nutmeg

Instructions:

Begin by gathering your bubbling cauldron, or in more mundane terms, a large pot. Pour in the cranberry juice and apple cider, letting these two mingle like old friends at a Halloween gathering. Next, introduce the fresh orange juice and brown sugar to the mix, stirring gently to dissolve the sweetness into this enchanting brew.

Now, it's time to spice things up. Add the cinnamon stick and whole cloves, those tiny but mighty wonders, into the pot. These will infuse your cider with an aroma that dances through the air, inviting ghosts and goblins alike. Toss in the slices of orange, allowing them to float and infuse their citrusy charm.

Scatter the cranberries into the mixture, watching as they bob eagerly, like mischievous spirits on the surface. Sprinkle the ground nutmeg with a flourish, and then bring the potion to a gentle boil over medium heat. Once it reaches a bubbling crescendo, reduce the heat to low, letting it simmer for about 20 minutes. This is when the magic truly happens, as the flavors meld into a harmonious symphony.

As the cider simmers, the anticipation builds. Soon enough, your kitchen will be filled with the hauntingly delicious aroma of autumn. Once ready, remove the pot from heat and carefully strain the cider into mugs, leaving behind the spices and fruit.

Serve this spine-chilling concoction warm, perhaps with a cinnamon stick for an added touch of elegance. It's a drink to savor slowly, as the night unfolds and Halloween's mysteries reveal themselves.

"May this Creepy Cranberry Cider bring warmth to your heart and a twinkle to your eye as you gather around with loved ones, sharing tales and laughter. Here's to magical moments and memories that linger long after the last sip is taken!

73. Zombie Zinger Lemonade

When the Halloween moon rises high and the little monsters start their trick-or-treating, why not surprise them with a chilling concoction that's both sweet and tangy? This Zombie Zinger Lemonade will add a splash of spooky fun to your festive gathering.

Preparation time: 10 minutes
Cooking time: 0 minutes
Ready-in time: 10 minutes
Serving size: 4 people

Ingredients:
4 cups of cold water
1 cup of freshly squeezed lemon juice
1/2 cup of honey
A few drops of green food coloring
1 lime, thinly sliced
1/4 cup of gummy worms
Ice cubes
Mint leaves for garnish

Instructions:

Start by gathering your ingredients; it's always best to have everything at the ready. In a large pitcher, combine the cold water and freshly squeezed lemon juice. Stir in the honey until it dissolves completely— think of it as waking up the sweet spirit within your lemonade.

Now, here's where the magic happens: add just a few drops of green food coloring to the mix. Stir gently and watch the transformation into a ghoulishly delightful potion. Be cautious not to overdo it, unless you're going for a more monstrous shade.

Slice up a lime into thin, delicate rounds and add them to the pitcher, giving your lemonade a zesty twist. Toss in the gummy worms; they'll wriggle and float, adding a fun, creepy touch that kids will adore.

Before you pour, fill each glass with a generous handful of ice cubes. Pour the lemonade over the ice, letting the eerie green liquid cascade down. Garnish each glass with a fresh mint leaf for an aromatic finish that's sure to delight.

Gather your friends and family around, and let this Zombie Zinger Lemonade be the spirited centerpiece of your Halloween haunt. Just remember, the best potions are always brewed with a dash of fun and a pinch of creativity. Happy haunting!

74. Eerie Eyeball Elixir

On a night when the moon grins like a Cheshire cat, and little goblins and ghouls giggle in the shadows, conjure this tantalizing potion to delight and amuse. It's a bewitching blend that will have your little monsters clamoring for more!

Preparation time: 15 minutes
Cooking time: 5 minutes
Ready-in time: 20 minutes
Serving size: 4 people

Ingredients:
3 cups lychee juice
1 cup cranberry juice
1 cup lemon-lime soda
8 canned lychees, drained
8 blueberries
Ice cubes
Gummy worms, for garnish

Instructions:

Let's begin by creating our spooky eyeballs. Take your drained lychees—those pale, round fruits that look eerily like eyeballs—and gently tuck a plump blueberry into the center of each one. Now, set them aside on a plate while we prepare the potion.

In a large pitcher, pour in the lychee juice, which gives our elixir a mysterious sweetness. Next, add the cranberry juice, its deep red hue reminiscent of the twilight hour. Stir these juices together with care, as if you were mixing a magical brew.

Now, for a touch of effervescence, slowly pour in the lemon-lime soda. The bubbles dance and swirl, adding a lively touch to our concoction. Stir gently, just as a witch would stir her cauldron.

Fill four tall glasses with ice cubes, creating a frosty base for our elixir. Carefully pour the juice mixture over the ice, allowing the chilling effect to enhance the flavors.

Finally, place two lychee-blueberry eyeballs into each glass, letting them float like eerie orbs in the potion. For an extra touch of whimsy, drape a gummy worm over the rim of each glass.

And there you have it, a ghoulishly delightful Eerie Eyeball Elixir!

Gather your little witches and wizards, and let the festivities begin. With each sip, they'll be enchanted, and perhaps even inspired to concoct their own magical brews. Remember, the best spells are shared with those you love!

75. Wicked Watermelon Cooler

When the moon is high and the air is thick with mystery, there's nothing quite like a refreshing potion to quench your thirst. This Wicked Watermelon Cooler casts a spell of delight with its vibrant hue and tantalizing taste—perfect for a bewitching Halloween gathering.

Preparation time: 15 minutes
Cooking time: 0 minutes
Ready-in time: 15 minutes
Serving size: 4 people

Ingredients:
3 cups watermelon, cubed and chilled
1 cup fresh strawberries, hulled
1 cup coconut water
2 tablespoons honey
Juice of 1 lime
1/4 teaspoon sea salt
Ice cubes
Fresh mint leaves for garnish

Instructions:

Begin by gathering your ingredients, ensuring your watermelon is sweet and juicy. In the spirit of creativity, take your cubed watermelon and strawberries, and place them into a blender. Add the coconut water, which will lend a tropical flair to our potion. Spoon in the honey for a touch of sweetness, and squeeze in the lime juice to add a zesty kick. Sprinkle in the sea salt, a secret ingredient that enhances the flavors beautifully.

Now, blend this magical mixture until it's completely smooth, conjuring a delightful pink hue that's sure to enchant. If the mixture is too thick for your liking, simply add a splash more of coconut water to achieve the perfect consistency.

Once blended, strain the cooler through a fine sieve to ensure a silky-smooth texture, discarding any pulp. Fill four glasses with ice cubes, and pour this elixir over the top, watching the colors swirl like a witch's cauldron.

Finally, garnish each glass with a fresh mint leaf, gently pressing it to release its aromatic essence. Serve immediately, and watch as your guests are spellbound by this refreshing brew.

May this Wicked Watermelon Cooler cast a spell of joy and laughter over your Halloween festivities. Remember, a touch of creativity and a dash of imagination are the key ingredients to any magical gathering. Cheers to a hauntingly delightful celebration!

76. Skeleton Shake

In the world of Halloween enchantment, even the simplest concoctions can take on a life of their own. This ghoulishly delightful Skeleton Shake is where whimsy meets a touch of spookiness, making it the perfect potion for little trick-or-treaters and grown-up ghouls alike.

Preparation time: 10 minutes
Cooking time: 0 minutes
Ready-in time: 10 minutes
Serving size: 4 people

Ingredients:
2 cups vanilla ice cream
1 cup milk
4 tablespoons chocolate syrup
1 teaspoon vanilla extract
1/2 cup whipped cream
Mini marshmallows for garnish
Black licorice strings for garnish
Candy eyeballs for garnish

Instructions:

Let's begin our ghostly culinary adventure by gathering our ingredients and a blender. Scoop two cups of vanilla ice cream, creamy and cold, into the pitcher of your blender. To that, add a cup of milk. I prefer whole milk for its richness, but feel free to adjust to your family's tastes.

Now, for a dash of excitement, pour in four tablespoons of chocolate syrup. This will give our shake its eerie, dark hue. A teaspoon of vanilla extract follows, enhancing the sweet symphony that's about to ensue.

Secure the lid of your blender tightly and blend until smooth. You're aiming for a consistency that is thick enough to hold our spooky garnishes, yet smooth enough to sip delightfully through a straw.

Once blended to perfection, pour your Skeleton Shake into four tall glasses. Now, the fun begins! Swirl a generous dollop of whipped cream atop each shake, forming the base for our skeleton faces.

Carefully place mini marshmallows atop the whipped cream to form ghostly bones, then adorn with candy eyeballs for an unsettling stare. Finally, use black licorice strings to create a haunting grin or spooky skeleton mouth.

Serve immediately and watch as your guests are spellbound by this ghoulishly good treat.

Ah, the Skeleton Shake, it's not just a drink, but a delightful dance of flavors and fun! Perfect for those who enjoy a playful twist on the classic milkshake. Remember, the trick to a great Halloween is a treat like this one!

77. Frightening Fruit Fizz

As the moonlight dances over your Halloween gathering, delight your guests with a potion as mysterious as it is delicious. This Frightening Fruit Fizz is a bubbling concoction that will enchant both the young and the young-at-heart.

Preparation time: 10 minutes
Cooking time: 0 minutes
Ready-in time: 10 minutes
Serving size: 4 people

Ingredients:
2 cups sparkling water
1 cup pomegranate juice
1 cup orange juice
1/2 cup fresh lime juice
1/4 cup grenadine
1/2 cup fresh blueberries
1/2 cup fresh raspberries
1/4 cup blackberries
Ice cubes
Optional: gummy worms or creepy candy for garnish

Instructions:

Begin by gathering your cauldron—or, in this case, a large pitcher. Pour in the sparkling water, which will serve as the base of our magical brew. Next, slowly add in the pomegranate juice, letting its deep red hue swirl and blend intriguingly with the bubbles. Follow this with the bright and sunny orange juice, which brings a touch of warmth to our eerie elixir.

Now, it's time to introduce a tartness with the fresh lime juice. Squeeze the limes with a gentle twist to extract every last drop of their zesty essence. Add in the grenadine, allowing it to weave in scarlet ribbons that will thrill any onlooker.

With the liquid elements mixed, introduce a handful of fresh blueberries and raspberries. These will float atop the fizz, like mysterious orbs suspended in a bubbly abyss. Toss in a scattering of blackberries for a touch of darkness, adding an air of mystery to the drink.

Fill serving glasses with ice cubes, then gently pour in the Frightening Fruit Fizz. For an extra touch of whimsy, perch a gummy worm or two on the rim of each glass.

With your Frightening Fruit Fizz now complete, watch as your guests sip and savor, delighting in the flavors that are as enchanting as a witch's spell. May your Halloween be filled with laughter, delight, and just the right amount of fright!

78. Mummy's Minty Mocktail

As the Halloween moon glows eerily bright, there's nothing quite as refreshing as a minty concoction to delight both young ghosts and ghouls. This tantalizing mocktail is as cool as a mummy's tomb and as sweet as your favorite trick-or-treat candy.

Preparation time: 10 minutes
Cooking time: None
Ready-in time: 10 minutes
Serving size: 4 people

Ingredients:
2 cups of sparkling water
1/2 cup of fresh mint leaves
1/4 cup of lime juice
1/4 cup of simple syrup
Ice cubes
Mint sprigs for garnish
Lime slices for garnish

Instructions:

Let's begin by assembling our ingredients like a skilled potion master. First, take the fresh mint leaves and gently muddle them in a mixing bowl. This releases their delightful aroma and flavor, which is the soul of our mocktail. Now, in a pitcher, combine the muddled mint, lime juice, and simple syrup. Stir this mixture with care, as if you're stirring a cauldron of sweet enchantment.

Next, pour in the sparkling water, observing as it bubbles and fizzes like a witch's brew. Add a handful of ice cubes to the pitcher, giving our concoction an icy chill reminiscent of a mummy's touch.

Now, it's time to serve. Take four glasses and fill each one with the minty mixture, straining out the muddled mint leaves. For an extra dash of Halloween spirit, garnish each glass with a sprig of fresh mint and a slice of lime. These final touches transform our mocktail into a work of art, ready to be enjoyed by all ages.

"Set your table with this minty delight, and watch as it casts a refreshing spell over your Halloween festivities. With each sip, you'll be transported to a world of whimsy and wonder, where mummies dance under the moonlight and magic fills the night air.

79. Pumpkin Potion Latte

When the leaves start to turn and the air crisps with the promise of autumn, there's nothing more enchanting than a warm, spiced beverage to wrap your hands around. This Pumpkin Potion Latte will brew a little magic into your day, casting a spell of comfort and delight.

Preparation time: 10 minutes
Cooking time: 10 minutes
Ready-in time: 20 minutes
Serving size: 4 people

Ingredients:
2 cups milk
2 tablespoons pumpkin puree
1 tablespoon sugar
1 tablespoon vanilla extract
1 teaspoon pumpkin pie spice
1 cup strong brewed coffee
Whipped cream, for topping
Ground cinnamon, for garnish

Instructions:

Let's begin our potion-making by gently heating the milk in a saucepan over medium heat. We want it warm, not boiling. While that's warming up, whisk in the pumpkin puree. You'll know it's ready when the mixture is smooth and slightly thickened. Now, add the sugar, stirring until it dissolves completely.

Next, invite the vanilla extract and pumpkin pie spice to join the cauldron. Stir them in until the mixture is fragrant and well-combined. Now, it's time to add the brewed coffee, pouring it in with a steady hand. Stir everything together, and allow the flavors to meld for a moment.

Once your potion is ready, divide it carefully into four mugs. Top each with a generous dollop of whipped cream, and give a light dusting of cinnamon for that magical touch.

Serve your Pumpkin Potion Latte warm, and watch as it delights the senses, leaving your guests enchanted and comforted.

"May your fall gatherings be as cozy and delightful as this Pumpkin Potion Latte. As the days grow shorter, let this comforting brew remind you of the joy in simple pleasures and the magic found in everyday moments. Here's to a warm and wonderful season!

80. Black Cat Brew

In the spirit of Halloween, let's embark on a whimsical journey into the world of potions and brews. This enchanting Black Cat Brew is a delightful concoction that will captivate both the young and the young at heart. It's a deliciously spooky treat that's purr-fect for your Halloween festivities.

Preparation time: 10 minutes
Cooking time: 5 minutes
Ready-in time: 15 minutes
Serving size: 4 people

Ingredients:
2 cups grape juice
1 cup sparkling water
1/4 cup fresh lime juice
2 tablespoons honey
1 teaspoon activated charcoal powder
Ice cubes
4 black licorice sticks

Instructions:

Let's begin by gathering all our ingredients. First, pour the grape juice into a large pitcher. The rich, purple hue is just the start of our mysterious brew. Next, add the sparkling water. The bubbles will give your potion an effervescent charm.

Into this fizzy mixture, gently stir in the fresh lime juice. The citrus adds a tangy note that balances the sweetness. Now, it's time for a touch of magic: drizzle in the honey. This golden nectar will blend beautifully with the other flavors.

The pièce de résistance, of course, is the activated charcoal powder. Carefully sprinkle it into the mixture, watching as the brew transforms into a deep, mysterious black. Stir gently until everything is well combined.

Prepare your serving glasses by filling them with ice cubes. Pour the Black Cat Brew over the ice, letting the chill enhance the flavors. Finally, for a whimsical touch, place a black licorice stick in each glass. It doubles as a straw and a playful garnish.

And there you have it—a brew that's as enchanting as it is delicious. Serve immediately and watch as your guests delight in this spooky, yet delightful treat.

May your Halloween be filled with laughter and joy as you sip on this magical brew. Enjoy the festivities, and remember, the best treats are those shared with family and friends. Until next time, may your days be as sweet as this enchanting potion!

81. Ghostly Granola Bars

As the leaves turn and the air grows crisp, it's time to embrace the spooky season with treats that delight and surprise. These Ghostly Granola Bars are a fun way to bring a touch of Halloween magic to your kitchen, perfect for little goblins and grown-up ghouls alike.

Preparation time: 15 minutes
Cooking time: 25 minutes
Ready-in time: 40 minutes
Serving size: 4 people

Ingredients:
1 1/2 cups rolled oats
1/2 cup almond butter
1/3 cup honey
1/4 cup pumpkin seeds
1/4 cup dried cranberries
1/4 cup mini marshmallows
1/2 teaspoon vanilla extract
1/4 teaspoon cinnamon
A pinch of salt
1/4 cup white chocolate chips, melted

Instructions:

To begin our ghostly adventure, preheat your oven to 350°F (175°C). While it warms, let's gather our ingredients and set the stage for a delightful creation. In a large mixing bowl, combine the rolled oats, pumpkin seeds, dried cranberries, and that small pinch of salt. Give it all a good stir to ensure even distribution.

Next, in a saucepan over medium heat, gently warm the almond butter and honey, stirring until they become one harmonious mixture. Once perfectly blended, remove from heat and add the vanilla extract and cinnamon for a hint of warmth and fragrance.

Now, pour the liquid gold over the dry ingredients and mix until every oat and seed is lovingly coated. Transfer this sticky concoction into a parchment-lined baking pan, pressing it firmly to ensure it sets beautifully.

Bake in your preheated oven for about 20 to 25 minutes, or until the edges are just golden. Once baked, remove from the oven and let cool slightly before adding the final touch.

Drizzle the melted white chocolate over the top, and while it is still warm, place the mini marshmallows strategically to resemble ghostly apparitions. Allow the chocolate to set, then cut into bars and prepare to be enchanted.

These bars are not just treats; they're a delightful trip into the whimsies of Halloween. Enjoy the smiles and spooky stories they inspire, and may your home be filled with laughter and a touch of eerie excitement this season. Boo-tifully delicious, aren't they?

82. Bewitched Bagel Faces

Ah, the magical allure of Halloween! When the moon is high and the air is crisp, these bewitching bagel faces will bring a sprinkle of enchantment to your family kitchen. Crafted with love and a touch of whimsy, they're sure to delight both young and old alike.

Preparation time: 20 minutes
Cooking time: 10 minutes
Ready-in time: 30 minutes
Serving size: 4 people

Ingredients:
4 plain bagels, halved
8 tablespoons cream cheese
4 black olives, sliced
1 red bell pepper, cut into triangles
1 small cucumber, sliced into rounds
1 carrot, peeled and sliced into thin rounds
16 mini pepperoni slices
4 cherry tomatoes, halved

Instructions:

Let's begin by toasting those bagel halves until they're golden and crispy. While they're getting a little warmth, prepare your creative palette of ingredients. Spread each toasted bagel half generously with two tablespoons of creamy, dreamy cream cheese. This will be the canvas for your masterpiece.

Now, let's bring these faces to life. Begin with the eyes: place two cucumber slices on each bagel, and crown them with a slice of black olive for pupils. Feel free to adjust them to give each face its unique expression. For a dash of mischievous charm, use the carrot rounds as cheeks, adding a rosy glow to your bagel faces.

Next, position the red bell pepper triangles as noses. These add a pop of color and a hint of spookiness. For that cheeky smile, line up four mini pepperoni slices in a curve below the nose—this will surely make your bagels grin with delight.

Finally, top each face with a halved cherry tomato as a jaunty hat or a quirky hairdo. Now, step back and admire your bewitching creations.

"Gather your little goblins and witches around the table, and let these Bewitched Bagel Faces cast a spell of laughter and delight. Who knew breakfast could be this much fun? Until next time, keep your kitchen filled with magic and merriment!

83. Creepy Crawly Pancakes

On a misty Halloween morning, when the air is filled with the promise of enchantment, what could be more delightful than crafting a breakfast that's as playful as it is delicious? Enter the Creepy Crawly Pancakes—guaranteed to bring smiles and perhaps a few gasps of glee to your family's faces.

Preparation time: 15 minutes
Cooking time: 20 minutes
Ready-in time: 35 minutes
Serving size: 4 people

Ingredients:
1 ½ cups all-purpose flour
3 ½ teaspoons baking powder
1 tablespoon sugar
½ teaspoon salt
1 ¼ cups milk
1 egg
3 tablespoons melted butter
Black food coloring
Green food coloring
Chocolate syrup
Mini marshmallows
Candy eyes

Instructions:

Begin by whisking together the dry ingredients: flour, baking powder, sugar, and salt. In a separate bowl, combine the milk, egg, and melted butter, whisking until they come together smoothly. Now, gently fold the wet ingredients into the dry, stirring until just combined. Divide the batter into two bowls. To one bowl, add a few drops of black food coloring and to the other, a few drops of green, stirring each until you achieve a vibrant color.

Heat a non-stick skillet over medium heat and lightly grease it with butter. Pour a small ladleful of the black batter onto the pan, forming a spooky spider shape. Repeat with the green batter, crafting eerie caterpillars or ghastly ghosts. Cook until bubbles form on the surface, then flip and cook until golden on the underside, about 2-3 minutes per side.

Arrange your creepy creations on a platter, drizzling them with chocolate syrup to create spider webs or caterpillar trails. Dot them with mini marshmallows and candy eyes for a ghoulish gaze. Serve immediately, and watch as the magic of Halloween comes alive at your breakfast table.

Ah, the simple pleasures of a morning spent in the company of deliciously eerie pancakes. May your Halloween be filled with laughter and perhaps, just a little mischief. Enjoy every bite of this whimsical feast, and remember, sometimes the best memories are made with a touch of the unexpected.

84. Spooky Spiderweb Waffles

As autumn leaves crunch underfoot and whispers of whimsy fill the crisp air, it's time to weave a breakfast spell that delights both the young and young at heart. These spiderweb waffles are the perfect blend of eerie charm and delectable delight, perfect for a Halloween morning surprise.

Preparation time: 15 minutes
Cooking time: 20 minutes
Ready-in time: 35 minutes
Serving size: 4 people

Ingredients:
2 cups all-purpose flour
2 tablespoons sugar
1 tablespoon baking powder
1/2 teaspoon baking soda
1/4 teaspoon salt
2 large eggs
1 3/4 cups buttermilk
1/3 cup unsalted butter, melted
1 teaspoon vanilla extract
Black food coloring
Powdered sugar, for dusting
Chocolate syrup, for spiderweb design

Instructions:

Begin by whisking together the flour, sugar, baking powder, baking soda, and salt in a large mixing bowl. It's like creating a magical powder that will soon transform into a delicious treat. In a separate bowl, lightly beat the eggs, then add the buttermilk, melted butter, and vanilla extract. Stir these liquid ingredients gently, ensuring they're well combined, but remember, no need to rush—let the flavors mingle.

Now comes the fun part: combining the wet and dry ingredients. Pour the liquid mixture into the dry, stirring just until everything comes together. Be careful not to overmix; we want our waffles tender and light. Divide the batter in half, and in one portion, add a few drops of black food coloring. Mix until the color is evenly distributed.

Preheat your waffle iron. Once hot, lightly grease with cooking spray. Pour a small amount of the black batter in the center, then spoon the regular batter around it to create a web-like effect. Cook until the waffle is golden and crisp, about 3-4 minutes.

Once all your waffles are ready, it's time to decorate. Use chocolate syrup to draw spiderweb patterns on each waffle, and dust lightly with powdered sugar for a gossamer effect.

With these spiderweb waffles, your Halloween breakfast will be the talk of the cauldron! Watch as little ghosts and ghouls gather 'round for a taste of this spooky delight, where every bite is a trick and a treat. Enjoy, and may your Halloween be as enchanting as these waffles!

85. Monster Muffins

Who says Halloween treats can't be monstrously delicious and delightfully spooky at the same time? These charming Monster Muffins are crafted to captivate the imagination of both young and old, bringing a splash of whimsical fun to your festive table.

Preparation time: 20 minutes
Cooking time: 25 minutes
Ready-in time: 45 minutes
Serving size: 4 people

Ingredients:
1 and 3/4 cups all-purpose flour
1/2 cup granulated sugar
1/4 cup unsweetened cocoa powder
2 teaspoons baking powder
1/4 teaspoon salt
1/2 cup milk
1/3 cup vegetable oil
1 large egg
1 teaspoon vanilla extract
1/2 cup mini chocolate chips
Assorted candy eyes
Colored frosting or icing pens

Instructions:

Begin by preheating your oven to a cozy 350°F (175°C). Line a muffin tin with paper liners, and let's embark on this fantastical baking adventure. In a large mixing bowl, whisk together the flour, sugar, cocoa powder, baking powder, and salt. This dry mixture forms the very foundation of our monster creations.

In a separate bowl, blend the milk, vegetable oil, egg, and vanilla extract until smooth and harmonious. Pour the wet ingredients into the dry, and gently fold them together until just combined. Remember, a few lumps are perfectly acceptable – they add character!

Now, sprinkle in those delightful mini chocolate chips, distributing them evenly throughout the batter like little treasures hidden by mischievous goblins. Divide the batter evenly among the muffin cups, filling each about two-thirds full.

It's time for these muffins to transform in the oven for 20 to 25 minutes. You'll know they're ready when a toothpick inserted into the center emerges clean, much like a wizard's wand casting a successful spell.

Once cooled, the real magic begins. Use colorful frosting or icing pens to decorate your muffins with amusing monster faces. Stick on those candy eyes, and allow your creativity to run wild.

Behold, you've conjured a batch of Monster Muffins that are sure to enchant and entertain! Share these delicious creatures with your family, and watch as their eyes light up with delight. Happy haunting and baking, dear friends!

86. Jack-O'-Lantern French Toast

As the crisp autumn air rustles through the golden leaves, let's turn breakfast into a delightful masterpiece that captures the essence of Halloween. Transform your kitchen into a creative workshop where each slice of bread becomes a whimsical canvas, bringing smiles to little faces with every bite.

Preparation time: 10 minutes
Cooking time: 15 minutes
Ready-in time: 25 minutes
Serving size: 4 people

Ingredients:
8 slices of thick white bread
4 large eggs
1 cup whole milk
2 tablespoons granulated sugar
1 teaspoon pure vanilla extract
1 teaspoon ground cinnamon
Butter, for frying
Powdered sugar, for dusting
Maple syrup, for serving
Orange food coloring
Chocolate chips or raisins, for decoration

Instructions:

To begin our Jack-O'-Lantern adventure, gather those plump slices of white bread and carve out whimsical jack-o'-lantern faces using a small paring knife. Don't fret about perfection; each face should have its own character, just like a real pumpkin patch.

Next, in a shallow bowl, whisk together the eggs, milk, sugar, vanilla extract, and cinnamon until blended into a frothy concoction. Add a few drops of orange food coloring to give your egg mixture a delightful pumpkin hue.

Preheat a large skillet over medium heat and melt a pat of butter until it sizzles, painting the pan with buttery goodness. Dip each slice of bread into the egg mixture, ensuring it's well-coated but not overly soggy.

Place the slices onto the hot skillet, cooking each side for about 3 to 4 minutes, until golden and slightly crisp. As they cook, admire the way your kitchen fills with the comforting aroma of cinnamon and vanilla.

Once cooked to perfection, transfer your Jack-O'-Lantern French Toast to a serving platter. Add chocolate chips or raisins to craft eyes and noses, bringing your delightful creations to life. Dust with a sprinkle of powdered sugar for a touch of magic and serve with a generous drizzle of maple syrup.

Now, as you gather around the breakfast table, let these charming Jack-O'-Lantern French Toast slices ignite the spirit of creativity and autumnal joy. May this enchanting recipe become a cherished tradition, weaving memories as rich and warm as the colors of fall.

87. Sinister Smoothie Bowl

In the spirit of Halloween, let's concoct a delightfully eerie smoothie bowl that beckons with vibrant colors and tantalizing flavors. Perfect for a spooky breakfast or a ghoulish snack, this creation will enchant little goblins and adult specters alike, bringing a touch of magic to your table.

Preparation time: 15 minutes
Cooking time: 0 minutes
Ready-in time: 15 minutes
Serving size: 4 people

Ingredients:
2 ripe bananas, frozen
1 cup frozen mixed berries (such as blueberries, blackberries, and raspberries)
1 cup spinach leaves
1 cup almond milk
1 tablespoon honey
1 teaspoon vanilla extract
1 tablespoon chia seeds
1 tablespoon pumpkin seeds
1/4 cup granola
1 kiwi, peeled and sliced
1/4 cup blackberries
Edible eyes or candy eyes for decoration

Instructions:

Begin by assembling your ingredients, giving a nod to the whimsical nature of Halloween. In your blender, combine the frozen bananas and mixed berries—these will lend our smoothie bowl its rich, mysterious hue. Add the spinach leaves for a dash of green that'll secretly infuse some goodness into our creation.

Now, pour in the almond milk, letting it cascade over the fruits and greens like a bubbling potion. Add the honey and vanilla extract, whispering a spell of sweetness into the mix. Blend these ingredients to a smooth, creamy consistency that resembles a witch's brew.

Once blended, gently stir in the chia seeds, letting them swell and add texture to your smoothie. Pour the mixture into bowls, creating a canvas for your sinister toppings.

Artfully arrange the pumpkin seeds, granola, kiwi slices, and blackberries atop the smoothie's surface. These elements will provide a delightful crunch and burst of flavor with every bite. Finally, place the edible eyes in strategic spots, ensuring that your creation gazes back at its beholder with a playful, mischievous stare.

And there you have it—a Sinister Smoothie Bowl that's as enchanting as it is delicious.

Gather your little monsters and watch as they delight in this hauntingly fun treat. Remember, the true magic of Halloween lies in the joy of creating something wickedly wonderful together. Until next time, may your culinary adventures be as thrilling as a moonlit night!

88. Vampire Veggie Omelette

As the misty moonlight spills through your kitchen window, gather your ingredients for this delightfully spooky omelette. Perfect for a Halloween brunch, this dish brings the colorful crunch of fresh vegetables to your table, delighting ghouls and goblins of all ages.

Preparation time: 15 minutes
Cooking time: 10 minutes
Ready-in time: 25 minutes
Serving size: 4 people

Ingredients:
6 large eggs
1/4 cup milk
Salt and pepper to taste
2 tablespoons olive oil
1 small red bell pepper, diced
1/2 cup baby spinach, chopped
1/4 cup red onion, finely chopped
1/4 cup mushrooms, sliced
1/2 cup shredded mozzarella cheese
1/4 teaspoon smoked paprika
Ketchup or hot sauce for garnish

Instructions:

Let's begin this enchanting culinary journey by cracking the eggs into a medium-sized bowl. Add the milk, a pinch of salt, and a dash of pepper. Whisk them together with a gentle, rhythmic motion until they're perfectly combined and frothy.

Next, heat a tablespoon of olive oil in a non-stick skillet over medium heat. As the oil shimmers, add the red bell pepper, baby spinach, red onion, and mushrooms. Sauté these colorful veggies, stirring occasionally, until they become tender and fragrant. This should take about 5 minutes.

In a separate skillet, warm the remaining tablespoon of olive oil over medium heat. Pour in the whisked eggs, ensuring they spread evenly across the pan. Allow the eggs to cook undisturbed for about 2 minutes, until the edges start to set.

Sprinkle the sautéed veggies and mozzarella cheese over half of the omelette. Using a spatula, carefully fold the other half over the filling, creating a delightful pocket of flavors.

Reduce the heat to low and cover the skillet for another 2-3 minutes, allowing the cheese to melt to oozy perfection. Once done, slide the omelette onto a serving platter.

For a spooky twist, drizzle ketchup or hot sauce in a zigzag pattern across the omelette, reminiscent of a vampire's bite. Serve immediately, and watch as your family devours this deliciously eerie creation.

And there you have it, a breakfast fit for a family of friendly vampires. Remember, even the simplest meal can become an extraordinary experience with a touch of creativity and a sprinkle of seasonal magic. Bon appétit, and happy haunting!

89. Haunted Hash Browns

As the crisp autumn air begins to weave its magic, transforming each leaf into a tapestry of gold and crimson, our kitchens become the heart of enchantment. What better way to celebrate the season than by crafting these whimsical Haunted Hash Browns, a delightfully spooky treat for your little goblins.

Preparation time: 15 minutes
Cooking time: 20 minutes
Ready-in time: 35 minutes
Serving size: 4 people

Ingredients:
2 large russet potatoes, peeled
1 small onion, finely chopped
1/4 cup all-purpose flour
1 large egg, beaten
Salt and pepper, to taste
1/2 teaspoon garlic powder
1/2 teaspoon smoked paprika
4 tablespoons olive oil
Black olives, sliced (for eyes)
Ketchup (for spooky details)

Instructions:

Begin by grating the russet potatoes using the large holes of a box grater. Now, this is a bit of elbow grease, but oh, the results are worth it. Place the grated potatoes in a clean kitchen towel and squeeze out as much moisture as you can—this is crucial for achieving that delightful crispness.

In a large mixing bowl, combine the grated potatoes with the finely chopped onion, all-purpose flour, beaten egg, a good pinch of salt, and a dash of pepper. Add in the garlic powder and smoked paprika, these spices add a wonderful depth, making our hash browns delightfully aromatic.

Next, heat the olive oil in a large non-stick skillet over medium heat. You'll need a gentle hand now, dividing the potato mixture into four equal portions, and shaping each one into a ghostly form—a little creativity here goes a long way!

Carefully place your potato ghosts into the skillet, cooking them for about 8-10 minutes on each side, until they're golden brown and hauntingly irresistible. Use a spatula to gently flip them, ensuring they keep their spooky shapes.

Once cooked, transfer your ghostly creations to a serving dish. Now, for the fun part—use the black olive slices to create eyes, and a few dots of ketchup to add eerie expressions.

"Gather your little monsters around and watch their eyes light up with delight as they devour these spectral treats. Remember, in the kitchen, it's the moments we create, the laughter we share, and the love we pour into each dish that truly matters. Happy haunting!

90. Phantom Fruit Parfaits

When the moon is full and the night is alive with whispers of enchantment, our kitchen transforms into a realm of creativity. With a sprinkle of magic and a dash of fun, we conjure these Phantom Fruit Parfaits, a treat as delightful as they are mysterious, perfect for your little ghouls and goblins.

Preparation time: 15 minutes
Cooking time: 0 minutes
Ready-in time: 15 minutes
Serving size: 4 people

Ingredients:
1 cup of vanilla Greek yogurt
1 cup of blackberries
1 cup of sliced strawberries
1 cup of kiwi slices
1/4 cup of honey
1 teaspoon of vanilla extract
1/2 cup of granola
1/4 cup of mini marshmallows
A few edible candy eyes

Instructions:

Let us begin by gathering all our ingredients, laying them out like a painter preparing a colorful palette. First, in a medium bowl, take the creamy vanilla Greek yogurt and blend it gently with the honey and vanilla extract. This creates a sweet, aromatic base for our parfaits.

Now, it's time to assemble the parfaits. Take four clear glasses or jars—presentation is key, after all, and we want to showcase our spectral delights. Begin by spooning a generous layer of the honey-vanilla yogurt into each glass.

Next, let the haunting hues of the fruits paint their magic. Add a layer of luscious blackberries, followed by a layer of vibrant strawberries. Top these with the green intrigue of kiwi slices, creating a vivid tapestry of flavors and colors.

For a bit of crunch, sprinkle a layer of granola over the fruit. Then, add another layer of the honey-vanilla yogurt, gently smoothing it with the back of your spoon.

To finish, scatter a few mini marshmallows on top, like little ghostly puffs, and place the edible candy eyes strategically amongst them. These will be the phantoms peeking out from their fruity lair.

And there you have it—a Phantom Fruit Parfait, ready to delight and enchant.

Embrace the whimsy and wonder of these spirited parfaits. With each spoonful, let the flavors dance upon your palate, conjuring smiles and laughter. Until next time, may your kitchen be a haven of creativity and joy, where every dish tells a story.

91. Witch's Brew Breakfast Burritos

On a crisp autumn morning, when the air is filled with whispers of enchantment, there's nothing quite like gathering around a warm breakfast that conjures a little magic of its own. These breakfast burritos, with a bewitching blend of flavors, are perfect for a family feast that's both fun and delightfully spooky.

Preparation time: 15 minutes
Cooking time: 20 minutes
Ready-in time: 35 minutes
Serving size: 4 people

Ingredients:
4 large flour tortillas
6 large eggs
1/4 cup whole milk
1/2 teaspoon salt
1/4 teaspoon black pepper
1 tablespoon butter
1 cup cooked and crumbled breakfast sausage
1/2 cup shredded cheddar cheese
1/4 cup finely chopped green onions
1/2 cup black beans, drained and rinsed
1/2 cup diced tomatoes
1/4 cup sour cream
1/4 cup salsa
1/4 cup chopped fresh cilantro

Instructions:

To begin, gather your ingredients, and let's weave a little morning magic together. In a medium bowl, crack open the eggs with care, and whisk them together with milk, salt, and pepper until they're wonderfully frothy. This airy mixture is the heart of our enchanting brew.

Over medium heat, melt the butter in a nonstick skillet. Gently pour in the egg mixture, stirring slowly with a spatula as the eggs begin to set. Add the crumbled sausage, allowing its savory aroma to mingle with the eggs. Toss in the cheddar cheese and green onions, folding them in until the cheese is delightfully melted.

Warm the tortillas briefly in a dry skillet or microwave, ensuring they're soft and pliable. Now, let's assemble our concoction: lay a tortilla flat, spoon a generous helping of the egg mixture down the center, and sprinkle with black beans and tomatoes. Roll it up snugly, tucking in the edges as you go.

Repeat this spellbinding process with the remaining tortillas. Serve with a dollop of sour cream, a drizzle of salsa, and a shower of fresh cilantro. Now, gather your family, and let the feast begin!

With each bite, may your day be filled with as much fun and flavor as our Witch's Brew Breakfast Burritos. Just remember, the only thing scary about these burritos is how quickly they disappear!

92. Ghastly Granola

As the autumn leaves rustle outside and the soft glow of jack-o'-lanterns flicker on the porch, nothing quite conjures the spirit of Halloween like a devilishly delicious snack. This Ghastly Granola will enchant your senses and delight both the young and the young at heart.

Preparation time: 10 minutes
Cooking time: 25 minutes
Ready-in time: 35 minutes
Serving size: 4 people

Ingredients:
2 cups rolled oats
1/2 cup pumpkin seeds
1/2 cup dried cranberries
1/4 cup slivered almonds
1/4 cup honey
1/4 cup maple syrup
2 tablespoons coconut oil
1 teaspoon vanilla extract
1/2 teaspoon cinnamon
1/4 teaspoon salt
1/4 teaspoon nutmeg
Pinch of allspice

Instructions:

Preheat your oven to 325°F (165°C), and imagine the sweet aroma that will soon fill your kitchen. In a large mixing bowl, combine the rolled oats, pumpkin seeds, dried cranberries, and slivered almonds. These are your frightful bits and pieces that will make up the body of our granola.

In a small saucepan over low heat, melt together the honey, maple syrup, and coconut oil until they become a luscious, golden potion. Stir in the vanilla extract, cinnamon, salt, nutmeg, and a pinch of allspice—these spices will conjure the warm, comforting notes of autumn.

Pour this aromatic liquid over your dry ingredients, and stir gently, ensuring every piece is cloaked in this magical elixir. Spread the mixture evenly on a baking sheet lined with parchment paper. Slide it into the preheated oven, and let it bake for 25 minutes, stirring halfway through to achieve an even, golden hue.

Once baked to perfection, remove the granola from the oven and let it cool completely. As it cools, the granola will crisp up, creating the perfect texture to crunch and munch.

Gather your little goblins and ghouls, and enjoy this Ghastly Granola while sharing tales of Halloween's past. Remember, in the kitchen, as in life, a little magic goes a long way. May your granola bring joy to your spooky festivities!

93. Eerie Egg Cups

As the moon casts its ghostly glow over your kitchen, dive into the whimsical world of witchery with these Eerie Egg Cups. A bewitching blend of flavors, they are sure to enchant your guests on any dark and stormy night, leaving them spellbound and craving more.

Preparation time: 15 minutes
Cooking time: 25 minutes
Ready-in time: 40 minutes
Serving size: 4 people

Ingredients:
4 large eggs
4 strips of bacon
4 slices of whole wheat bread
1/2 cup shredded cheddar cheese
1 tablespoon chives, finely chopped
Salt and pepper to taste
Butter for greasing
A dash of paprika for a spooky touch

Instructions:

Begin by preheating your oven to a cozy 375°F (190°C). As the warmth fills the room, gently grease a muffin tin with butter, ensuring each cup is well-coated for a seamless release. Now, let us turn our attention to the bacon. In a skillet over medium heat, cook the strips until they are just beginning to crisp, but still pliable. Set them aside to cool for a moment.

Next, take the slices of whole wheat bread and, using a rolling pin, flatten them to a thin canvas. Carefully press each slice into the muffin tin, creating a rustic bread cup. Line the inside of each cup with a strip of bacon, forming a delicious nest.

Crack an egg into each bacon-lined cup, taking care not to break the yolk — a delicate task worthy of a true artisan. Sprinkle a generous pinch of salt, a whisper of pepper, and a sprinkle of cheddar cheese over each egg, followed by a dash of paprika for a hauntingly beautiful finish.

Place the muffin tin in the oven and bake for approximately 20 to 25 minutes, until the eggs are just set and the cheese is bubbling with golden delight. Once baked to perfection, carefully remove the eerie creations from the oven, allowing them to cool for a short spell. Garnish with chives, and your Eerie Egg Cups are ready to bewitch and delight your guests.

Now, as you gather around to enjoy these spooky delights, may your Halloween feast be filled with laughter, ghostly tales, and memories that linger long after the last crumb is gone. Here's to a hauntingly delightful celebration!

94. Zombie Zucchini Bread

As the autumn air turns crisp and the leaves dance in a fiery ballet, what better way to celebrate the spooky season than with a loaf of Zombie Zucchini Bread? This ghoulishly delightful treat will awaken the monster in your taste buds, making it a Halloween hit for the whole family.

Preparation time: 15 minutes
Cooking time: 1 hour
Ready-in time: 1 hour 15 minutes
Serving size: 4 people

Ingredients:
1 ½ cups all-purpose flour
1 teaspoon baking powder
½ teaspoon baking soda
½ teaspoon salt
1 teaspoon ground cinnamon
½ teaspoon ground nutmeg
¾ cup granulated sugar
¼ cup packed brown sugar
1 large egg
¼ cup vegetable oil
¼ cup unsweetened applesauce
1 teaspoon vanilla extract
1 cup grated zucchini
½ cup chopped walnuts (optional)
Green food coloring (a few drops, if you dare)

Instructions:

Let's begin our spooky adventure by preheating the oven to 350°F (175°C). Grease a 9x5 inch loaf pan, ensuring your creation doesn't stick. In a large mixing bowl, whisk together the flour, baking powder, baking soda, salt, cinnamon, and nutmeg. Set this aromatic mixture aside for now.

In another bowl, blend the granulated sugar, brown sugar, and the egg until they form a smooth, harmonious mixture. Add in the vegetable oil, applesauce, and vanilla extract, stirring until well combined.

Now, let's introduce our star ingredient—the zucchini. Gently fold the grated zucchini into the wet mixture, adding a splash of green food coloring for a hauntingly fun twist. Gradually incorporate the dry ingredients into the wet mixture, stirring until just combined. If you're feeling adventurous, toss in a handful of walnuts for a bit of crunch.

Pour this vibrant, batter into your prepared loaf pan, and slide it into the oven. Bake for about 1 hour, or until a toothpick inserted into the center comes out clean. Allow your Zombie Zucchini Bread to cool in the pan for a few minutes before transferring it to a wire rack to cool completely.

Whether you're sharing this eerie delight with family or friends, beware— its hauntingly good flavor might just resurrect your inner chef! Enjoy every bite, and remember, the best treats are made with love and a dash of spooky fun.

95. Pumpkin Patch Porridge

Amidst the rustling leaves and the whispering winds of October, there's nothing quite as comforting as a steaming bowl of porridge that captures the essence of the pumpkin patch. This delightful dish will whisk your family away on a magical, autumnal morning adventure that even the littlest goblins will adore.

Preparation time: 10 minutes
Cooking time: 20 minutes
Ready-in time: 30 minutes
Serving size: 4 people

Ingredients:
1 cup rolled oats
2 cups milk (or a dairy-free alternative)
1 cup canned pumpkin puree
1 teaspoon pumpkin pie spice
2 tablespoons brown sugar
1 teaspoon vanilla extract
Pinch of salt
¼ cup chopped pecans
¼ cup dried cranberries
Honey or maple syrup, for drizzling

Instructions:

First, gather your ingredients with the same care as collecting precious jewels. In a medium saucepan, combine the rolled oats and milk. Bring them to a gentle simmer over medium heat, stirring occasionally to ensure they do not stick. As the oats begin to soften, add the pumpkin puree, pumpkin pie spice, brown sugar, vanilla extract, and a delicate pinch of salt. Stir the mixture with a wooden spoon, allowing the flavors to meld together like a harmonious autumn symphony.

Continue to cook the porridge for another 10 to 15 minutes, stirring frequently, until it reaches a creamy, luscious consistency. You'll know it's ready when it coats the back of your spoon like a velvet cloak.

Once the porridge is perfectly cooked, ladle it into four inviting bowls. Generously sprinkle each serving with chopped pecans and dried cranberries, adding a delightful crunch and a pop of color reminiscent of a vibrant pumpkin patch. For an extra touch of sweetness, drizzle with honey or maple syrup – a little goes a long way in enhancing the porridge's natural sweetness.

And there you have it: a perfect, seasonal breakfast that invites your family to gather around the table, sharing stories and savoring every spoonful.

May your mornings be filled with the warmth of pumpkin spice and the joy of shared moments. This porridge is a little bowl of happiness, perfect for starting a day filled with Halloween magic and cozy memories. Enjoy the simple pleasures of the season, one delightful bite at a time.

96. Frightening Frittata

In the enchanting glow of a Halloween morning, what could be more delightful than a frittata filled with the colors and flavors of fall? This spine-chilling dish is perfect for little goblins and ghouls eager to start their day with a spooky surprise.

Preparation time: 15 minutes
Cooking time: 30 minutes
Ready-in time: 45 minutes
Serving size: 4 people

Ingredients:
6 large eggs
1/4 cup whole milk
1/2 teaspoon salt
1/4 teaspoon black pepper
1 tablespoon olive oil
1 small red onion, thinly sliced
1 cup diced orange bell pepper
1 cup chopped spinach
1/2 cup cherry tomatoes, halved
1/2 cup shredded mozzarella cheese
1/4 cup grated Parmesan cheese
2 tablespoons fresh basil, chopped

Instructions:

Let's begin by preheating our oven to 375°F (190°C). While the oven warms up, crack the eggs into a large mixing bowl. Whisk them lightly, just until combined, then stir in the milk, salt, and pepper. Set this eggy mixture aside for a moment.

In a large, ovenproof skillet, heat the olive oil over medium heat. Add the sliced red onion and sauté until it becomes translucent and fragrant, about 3 minutes. Next, toss in the orange bell pepper and allow it to soften slightly, another 3 minutes should do. Now, add the spinach, stirring gently until it wilts.

With the vegetables nicely softened, pour the egg mixture over them. Give the skillet a gentle shake, ensuring the eggs spread evenly across the surface. Scatter the halved cherry tomatoes over the top, then sprinkle both cheeses evenly, allowing these to melt into a golden, bubbly topping.

Slide the skillet into your preheated oven and let the frittata bake for about 20 minutes, or until the eggs are set and the top is lightly browned. Once cooked, let it cool for a few minutes before sprinkling the fresh basil over the top. Slice into wedges and serve your Frightening Frittata warm.

Gather around the table and enjoy this whimsical creation, where each bite is a delightful reminder of Halloween magic. Remember, the joy of cooking is in experimenting and crafting unforgettable meals. Until next time, enjoy every spooky moment!

97. Mummy's Morning Muffins

In the soft glow of a fall morning, as the leaves crunch beneath our feet and the air turns crisp, transform your kitchen into a cauldron of creativity. These Mummy's Morning Muffins are a delightful way to greet the day with a whisper of Halloween magic and warmth.

Preparation time: 15 minutes
Cooking time: 20 minutes
Ready-in time: 35 minutes
Serving size: 4 people

Ingredients:
1 ½ cups all-purpose flour
1 teaspoon baking powder
½ teaspoon baking soda
½ teaspoon salt
½ cup granulated sugar
1 large egg
½ cup buttermilk
⅓ cup vegetable oil
1 teaspoon vanilla extract
1 cup grated apple
¼ cup mini chocolate chips
Candy eyeballs for decoration

Instructions:

Begin by preheating your oven to 350°F (175°C). Line a muffin tin with festive paper liners, setting the stage for our delightful creations. In a large mixing bowl, whisk together the flour, baking powder, baking soda, and salt. In a separate bowl, beat the sugar and egg until the mixture turns light and fluffy. Stir in the buttermilk, oil, and vanilla extract, blending until smooth and well-combined.

Now, gently fold the wet ingredients into the dry, taking care not to over-mix. The secret to tender muffins, after all, is a tender touch. Add the grated apple and mini chocolate chips, folding them into the batter with a few loving strokes.

Spoon the batter evenly into the prepared muffin cups, filling each about two-thirds full. As they bake, a delightful aroma will fill your kitchen, conjuring images of warm hugs and cozy mornings. Bake for 18 to 20 minutes, or until a toothpick inserted into the center of a muffin comes out clean. Allow the muffins to cool in the tin for a few minutes before transferring them to a wire rack.

Once cooled, add the final spooky touch by placing candy eyeballs on each muffin, transforming them into mummies ready to delight your little ghouls and goblins.

May your mornings be filled with mischief and muffins, and may each bite bring a smile to your face. Remember, the best kind of treat is the one shared with those you love most. Until next time, happy haunting and even happier baking!

98. Skull Shaped Scones

In the spirit of Halloween, we conjure up a treat that is both eerie and delightful! Imagine these skull-shaped scones gracing your table, lending a whimsical touch to your spooky festivities. They're not only a visual treat but also a delightful indulgence - a culinary delight certain to enchant all ages.

Preparation time: 20 minutes
Cooking time: 15 minutes
Ready-in time: 35 minutes
Serving size: 4 people

Ingredients:
2 cups all-purpose flour
1/4 cup granulated sugar
1 tablespoon baking powder
1/2 teaspoon salt
1/2 cup unsalted butter, cold and cubed
2/3 cup whole milk
1 large egg
1 teaspoon vanilla extract
1/2 cup mini chocolate chips

Instructions:

First, let's prepare our ingredients. Preheat your oven to a cozy 400°F (200°C) and line a baking sheet with parchment paper. In a large mixing bowl, whisk together the flour, sugar, baking powder, and salt, creating a harmonious blend of dry ingredients. Now, gently fold in the cold butter cubes, using your fingertips to rub the butter into the flour until the mixture resembles a coarse meal.

In a separate bowl, whisk together the milk, egg, and vanilla extract, combining them until smooth. Pour this mixture into the dry ingredients, stirring gently until just combined. Be mindful not to overmix, as we want our scones to be light and airy.

Now, fold in the chocolate chips, ensuring they're evenly distributed. On a lightly floured surface, roll out the dough to about an inch thick. Use a skull-shaped cookie cutter to cut out your scones, placing them on the prepared baking sheet. If you don't have a skull cutter, you can shape them by hand for a more rustic look.

Pop them into the preheated oven and bake for about 15 minutes, or until they are golden and risen. Allow them to cool slightly before serving, ensuring they are ready to be devoured.

With every bite, may your Halloween be filled with delightful moments and spooky joy. These skull-shaped scones are sure to become a family favorite, adding a touch of magic to your holiday tradition. Enjoy with a warm cup of cider or cocoa, and let the festivities begin!

99. Chilling Chia Pudding

As the autumn leaves begin to whisper secrets of fall and mist lingers like magic in the air, why not whip up a bewitching treat that delights both the eyes and the taste buds? This Chilling Chia Pudding is as eerie as it is scrumptious, casting a sweet spell on all who dare to indulge.

Preparation time: 5 minutes
Cooking time: 0 minutes
Ready-in time: 4 hours 5 minutes
Serving size: 4 people

Ingredients:
1 cup almond milk
1/4 cup chia seeds
2 tablespoons maple syrup
1 teaspoon vanilla extract
A pinch of cinnamon
1/4 cup crushed chocolate cookies
8 gummy worms
Green food coloring (optional)
1/4 cup whipped cream

Instructions:

Now, let's dive into our cauldron of creativity! Start with a medium-sized mixing bowl and pour in the almond milk. To this, add the chia seeds, and give it a good whisk. If you want to add a touch of the spooky, a drop or two of green food coloring will do the trick. The aim is for a light, ghostly hue.

Next, incorporate the maple syrup, vanilla extract, and a hint of cinnamon—these enchanting flavors will mingle beautifully as the pudding chills. Whisk again until the mixture is well combined.

Cover your potion with plastic wrap or a lid, and place it in the fridge for at least 4 hours, or overnight if possible. This time allows the chia seeds to work their magic, absorbing the liquid and thickening into a pudding-like consistency.

When the chilling is complete, stir the pudding once more and divide it among four serving glasses. Gently sprinkle the crushed chocolate cookies on top, creating the illusion of crumbled earth, and strategically place a couple of gummy worms in each glass for a ghoulish garnish. A dollop of whipped cream adds a final, whimsical touch.

Ah, there you have it—a delightfully eerie treat that promises to bring smiles and a touch of Halloween magic to your table. Whether it's a spooky soirée or a family gathering, this Chilling Chia Pudding is sure to enchant all who dare to taste. Enjoy, and may your Halloween be as sweet as it is spooky!

100. Wicked Waffle Sandwiches

In the haunted heart of the kitchen, where culinary magic brews, a mischievous breakfast awaits. These wicked waffle sandwiches promise to bewitch taste buds and delight ghoulish guests of all ages. A bewitching blend of sweet and savory, they're perfect for a spirited Halloween gathering.

Preparation time: 15 minutes
Cooking time: 10 minutes
Ready-in time: 25 minutes
Serving size: 4 people

Ingredients:
1 cup all-purpose flour
1 tablespoon granulated sugar
1 teaspoon baking powder
1/2 teaspoon baking soda
1/4 teaspoon salt
3/4 cup buttermilk
1/4 cup melted butter
1 large egg
1/2 teaspoon vanilla extract
4 slices cooked bacon
4 slices cheddar cheese
8 tablespoons pumpkin butter
2 tablespoons maple syrup

Instructions:

Let's begin our culinary enchantment by preheating your waffle iron to medium-high heat. In a large mixing bowl, whisk together flour, sugar, baking powder, baking soda, and salt. In another bowl, blend the buttermilk, melted butter, egg, and vanilla extract until the ingredients harmonize like a well-rehearsed spell. Gently fold the wet ingredients into the dry, stirring just until combined—no need to overmix, as we want our waffles to be light and airy.

Ladle the batter into your preheated waffle iron, spreading it evenly. Close the lid and let the magic happen. Cook until the waffles are golden brown and crisp to perfection, about 3 to 4 minutes. Once done, remove them carefully and place them on a cooling rack.

Now, let's assemble our wicked sandwiches. Spread a generous tablespoon of pumpkin butter on each waffle. Place a slice of cheddar cheese and a slice of crispy bacon on four of the waffles. Top each with another waffle, pumpkin butter side down, forming a delicious sandwich.

Finally, drizzle each sandwich with a touch of maple syrup, adding a sweet finish to our savory creation. Serve immediately, ensuring that each bite is as delightful as a moonlit Halloween night.

Gather around, young goblins and ghouls, as you savor these wicked delights. Each bite promises a playful blend of flavors that even the most discerning witches will adore. May your Halloween be as enchanting and delicious as these waffle wonders!

Thank you note and review request:

Thank you for joining me in the kitchen with *Creepy & Creative: 100 Fun Halloween Recipes for Kids and Families*. I hope these recipes brought as much joy, flavor, and festive fun to your home as they do to mine. There's nothing quite like creating memorable moments with loved ones over a beautifully prepared meal—especially one that captures the magic and whimsy of Halloween.

If you enjoyed the recipes and found them inspiring, I would greatly appreciate it if you shared your thoughts by leaving a review where you purchased the book. Your feedback is always valued.

And don't forget to explore my other collections for more culinary inspiration and timeless entertaining ideas.

Wishing you continued success and joy in the kitchen,

Josephine S. Stell

www.ingramcontent.com/pod-product-compliance
Lightning Source LLC
Chambersburg PA
CBHW071937150726
47999CB00001B/236